ARCHETYPES
MADE
EASY

BARBARA STONE-ANDREWS

Cover design by Deranged Doctor Design

Published by Journey of Awakening

Paperback ISBN: 978-0-9876452-1-0
Hardback ISBN: 978-0-9876452-2-7
Ebook ISBN: 978-0-9876452-0-3

 A catalogue record for this
book is available from the
National Library of Australia

DEDICATION

I dedicate this book to my twin sister Libby. Without you I wonder if I would still be here. I love you dearly. Thank you for sharing this interesting journey with me, from my heart to your heart, eternally.

To my wonderful husband Mark, thank you for your enduring love and support always.

To my beloved children, Adam, Lael and Garth, thank you for being you and together with your partners, Cath, Mike and Jess, giving me nine wonderful grandchildren.

To my many supportive and caring friends, particularly Robyn, Jenny and Justine, I love you and thank you for being a major part of my life, with your constant encouragement and contact.

Thank you Suzie for being the Divine Instrument in challenging me to get this book written and for encouraging me to bring the Chart Readings to the world.

Thank you to Maggie H, who approached me to write this book. You have held my hand along the way and I couldn't and wouldn't have done this without you.

Thank you to Elena Paige, who has been a guardian angel to come in and light the way to make this book into reality. You're a living treasure.

ARCHETYPES MADE EASY

TRANSFORM YOUR BELIEFS, EMPOWER YOUR
LIFE, LIVE YOUR TRUTH

BARBARA STONE-ANDREWS

Front cover painting by Dawn Miller.

The symbolism of the peacock is as follows:

Peacocks have a shimmering opalescence, with boisterous cries that hold a touch of laughter – as if to imply that no-thing, including beauty, should be taken too seriously. This helps remind us to stay centered on what is, and to be grateful for what we have. This is an important facet of wholeness. The peacock reminds us that true beauty comes from the inside. It also represents nobility, holiness, guidance, protection and Presence. It reminds us to show our true beauty to the world. The peacock is the closest in description to the mythical Phoenix, which rises, reborn, from the flames and ashes of its funeral pyre. The eyes on the peacock feathers represent their ability to see into the past, present and future. We need to look within for these gifts.

CONTENTS

INTRODUCTION

I started my self development journey around the age of twenty-seven. In astrological terms, this is called Saturn Return as this period in your life is meant to shake you up and may push you to do things differently in your life. Some of us get married, some start a new career, go overseas, or give birth. I remember wanting to understand how my mind worked, why we do what we do and what's the deeper meaning to life. Just little questions! So I started pursuing this pathway. Oh, I also decided to have a third child!

The world of Archetypes were working with me all the time, I just didn't know it back then. An Archetype is an overall term for different roles, patterns or behaviours that we play throughout our lives. We all play roles and we all develop patterns of behaviours throughout this journey. This may be due to our parents or culture giving us these patterns, like being the *Good Girl/Boy* Archetype, perhaps the *Pleaser* or *Rescuer* Archetype, maybe the High Achiever or the *Perfectionist* Archetype.

All too often these roles or behaviors limit us, so that we can feel negated by them in some way. If we have to be perfect all the time, then this sets up the body to experience high levels of internal stress that translates to physical illness as we get older, perhaps migraines or ulcers. These roles or behaviors are formed in our childhood, so we play them to stay safe or to be loved and approved of.

Having to be a *High Achiever* all the time means you are constantly comparing yourself to others and can set up beliefs that you're not good enough or not worthwhile, perhaps not clever enough. The flip side of this can also mean that you feel superior to others, perhaps better than them so you pity them for not being the same as you. All of these beliefs cause damage in some way or another.

One Archetype we all share is the *Victim*. This comes up when we feel hopeless and helpless, when things go wrong in our life and when we can't move in the direction we want to. This pattern is automatic for the majority of people on the planet. If we can understand these patterns or roles, then we become empowered to make other choices, to see life through a different lens and therefore open up to more choice and possibility.

Forty years down the track, I now understand how powerful Archetypes are when you use them consciously. It is liberating to be able to see what role is playing out, to understand where it is coming from and at what level of awareness.

There is a world of difference between the Archetype of the Victim at the Unconscious level and this Archetype at the Conscious level. The former does not take responsibility for anything that is happening in life and the latter takes full responsibility for it all and therefore becomes empowered to make change.

In 1996 I met Dr. Caroline Myss when I had the privilege of working with her for two intense weeks, in a small group of twenty-four people. Learning Caroline's unique way of working with Archetypes and how it was related to the astrological wheel, plus Carl Jung's Levels of Consciousness changed my life forever. I just "knew" this work, as it was easy for me to do (*Knower Archetype*). Caroline is a Master Teacher on the planet. I am eternally grateful to Spirit for guiding me to her. We both work differently around the Archetypal patterns as there's room for many ways of looking at the roles that shape our lives.

Now, over twenty thousand Archetype Chart Readings later, it is still the most powerful tool I have come across that reveals where you're at right now. It can show you what you're doing to hold yourself back and potentially, what needs to be done to shift old patterns that no longer serve you. It cuts to the chase very quickly.

I want to share this gift with you, so that you too can help yourself to be your highest possible potential, learn how to live from your heart, hopefully follow your intuition and truth and therefore open up to the vastness of your magnificent True Self.

For some of you, this book will challenge long held beliefs. That's ok, just imagine that you have three compartments available to you. One label says "Rubbish." The other is labelled "Possible," and the third one titled "Yes!"

Throw any of the ideas in this book into one of your compartments. I don't believe in right or wrong, good or bad, just wise and unwise behavior, or actions and consequences and the experience that goes with those choices.

Have fun with this, explore, play, and create. You will be given a lot of help along the way, as well as many resources to turn to and the opportunity to access videos on this work. My aim is to support you in this modality. Spirit guided this entire journey anyway so all thanks go to Source. I just had to show up and pay attention.

Please note that all clients' names have been changed to protect their identities, but the stories are real.

1

YOU ARE WHAT YOU BELIEVE

What if your life could change for the better? Would you want that? I imagine like most of us, you would. What then stops you from making these changes? Is it your current life circumstances? Are you feeling a little trapped right now? How is it for you? Is your health troubling you?

Are your relationships tricky? Maybe you keep on attracting in love relationships that betray you over and over again? You start off thinking this is it, then after a few years, it all turns sour and you end up back in the same place of being alone again?

Perhaps you're stuck in a job you hate, or feeling overwhelmed as you look after someone else. Your guilt says you must stay and help this person, as they won't cope without you! Have you run out of puff? Are you feeling a bit apathetic or your self-esteem, finances, fear of what others will think or family lineage has taken a dive? You cannot see how this situation can change for the better.

Or perhaps time is a big one for you? You simply don't have

enough hours in the day to do all that you want to. So you end up feeling exhausted and perhaps cheated? Do you find yourself without a moment to spare because you don't want to let others down? This can be as a result of believing that you'll only be loved if you serve others' needs (*Caretaker, Servant or Slave*).

If you're feeling a bit lost right now, then this book is here to guide you. It's important to know that all the situations mentioned above are due to beliefs that have been taught to you. This realisation may be huge for some of us, but it's true.

As a child, my parents impressed on me that the only role worth playing was to work hard all the time. As an adult, this exhausted me as I tried to become all things to all people. Of course, what I was playing was the classic *Good Girl/Pleaser/Servant* role. This meant doing what was asked of me, not rocking the boat and of course, no rebellion. At seventeen, I moved into an office job because that's what a good girl did and then I married at 20 (which was normal at that time).

The way to wake up was to end up with numerous illnesses in my life, and fortunately this made me look at this belief and examine if it was true! Of course I found out that it isn't true at all, that it's just a belief I had formed in my childhood to stay safe, loved and approved of.

I used to have a good friend called Kane. He learned very early never to make a decision in case it was wrong or it got him into trouble with authority figures. So all his life he would just play Mr Nice Guy, as he was good at it and indeed, he was a lovely man.

However, Kane was also not true to himself as his fear of speaking his real truth paralysed him. In fact, he often did not even know what his truth was! He usually just listened to others and rarely ventured an opinion. This is the way he stayed "safe," as he could never get it wrong or be criticized. He let people know him, but only at the surface level. He excelled at keeping everything inside, not showing his feelings or expressing them. Eventually, this took its toll on him physically and he became ill. He paid a high price for his acquiescence, through not dealing with his hurts and disappointments, to the extent that strong health issues came to the fore. He followed in his father's footsteps, whose behaviour was the same and from whom Kane had learned how to act and be in the world.

Even though we were good friends, Kane did not want to hear any alternative viewpoint, so he just stayed in his patterns and behaviors. Sometimes all you can do is just love the person who stays stuck because the fear of change is too great.

SO HOW DOES THIS LOOK FOR ME?

Once we start to see how our beliefs shape us, we've made an important first step. Too often in the past we do what we've always done, get upset and angry with the same people, disappointed in others, or ourselves, completely unaware that our beliefs impact the lives we lead. Added to that we don't have a school system that helps us examine these belief systems. The great news is that it doesn't have to be this way.

What if we were all raised in such a way that our first thought, whenever we were unsure, was to go to our own heart, asking the question: *"Is this action making my heart glow?"* Does this feel authentic to me? In fact, how am I feeling anyway? I wonder what choices we would make if this were our foundation. Can you imagine how this approach would transform much of what we do?

In the past, I have not had any boundaries in my life and one of the reasons I feel this is so is because I am an identical twin. Having people in my space is second nature to me. This has meant that I was not good at being clear with others and owning my true feelings. So my first reaction has always been to please others and put my own needs last. It actually never occurred to me that it could look another way.

Eventually, exhaustion and illness forced me to stop and evaluate my life and find out why I couldn't say no or why I always put myself last. From the age of ten, my shoulders started to partially dislocate. This meant that I had trouble dressing myself at times and doing certain things. Raising my arms was difficult plus the pain was chronic. My parents took me to many different medicos who offered many different treatments but nothing seemed to have a lasting effect. Unknowingly, I was addicted to pleasing others! Unknowingly I did not know how to say no. The need for approval from others was greater than my ability to go within and see what felt right for me.

I did not have a role model for this behavior either given that my parents were born around 1918. It wasn't until my mid thirties that I had a major epiphany and realised the core of my shoulder problem. I was addicted to carrying other people's burdens because I lacked healthy boundaries. It was like I had a sign out in my energy field that said: "Come and give me your problems as I'll take them on board for you!" I did this for about thirty-five years without realizing it of course. It did not vanish overnight either. It took quite a bit of practice for me to shift this old way of thinking and learn how to feel first and then speak later.

This is what the *Caretaker* looked like for me. It was a role I took on board to stay safe and valued. I didn't wake up one day and say I think I'll play this part for the rest of my life, it all happened at the sub-conscious level. It's not our real truth, but we play these roles so often that they become our truth because we identify with these different roles. We create our own reality this way, taking on board roles that will win us approval or love and have no idea that these roles can be damaging to us later down the track.

So I started an intense visualization process and a gratitude meditation regime to change this around. It worked and while my shoulders can still fatigue at times, I no longer have the pain. I have had to do this sort of work with many different parts of my body that have given me strong messages that my belief systems were not healthy for me. This includes my heart and lungs, kidneys, uterus, skin, bones, eyesight, shoulders, teeth, legs, ankles and gut issues just to name a few body parts and organs.

I have finally learned how to check in with my own heart first, to stop and feel into something, as opposed to answering from the automaticity of pleasing others.

Do you have clear boundaries? By this I mean are you easily able to stand in your truth and integrity and state what is important to you? Can you say NO with ease and grace, meaning without guilt or the fear that you will be rejected if you state your needs?

So many of us struggle with this because we were not allowed to speak our truth in our childhood. Most of us were not heard or had our feelings validated.

This means we can take on board different Archetypes or patterns to get our needs met. Roles such as *Good Girl, Pleaser, Rescuer, Helper, Healer, Servant, Slave, Scapegoat, Victim, Pros-*

titute, Child, Saboteur, Advocate, Maiden/Knight, Drama Queen plus many others.

When we have messy boundaries, we give out big mixed messages. We say "maybe" or "perhaps" instead of a clear NO. At this point on the planet, there is a lot of inappropriate sexual behaviour being made public. Gross misuse of power from the church, politicians, actors, CEO's, in fact in all walks of life.

Women have been afraid to say NO in case they hurt someone's feelings and therefore totally disregard their own feelings in the process. Some do say NO, but they're not heard, valued or honored because this is an age-old issue. In some cultures, women do not believe they have the right to say NO. Boys can be the target of abuse too, especially connected to the Church, which is an ultimate authority figure to young people.

One day all of this will change, but for now, it's work in progress for us ALL to learn we have to honor our feelings, our bodies, our boundaries and our sovereignty. It starts from within.

So what pushes your buttons? What happens when someone does something offensive or disagreeable to you? Do you become defensive or aggressive, shrink inside, or automatically go into self-doubt? Does fear arise in you the moment someone disagrees with you?

These reactions are showing us something, they're showing us that we hold onto strong beliefs and now would be a good time to examine what those beliefs are. While our values are sacrosanct to most of us, it's time to see if these values and beliefs come from a place of fear or love.

Kylie was caught up in the corporate world and earned a salary of two hundred thousand dollars plus. Her parents were very proud of her achievements and this motivated Kylie to just work harder and harder. However, her whole world was dominated by work and its incessant demands.

Kylie did not know how to get off this rollercoaster ride of continual stress, so eventually the body took over and rang major alarm bells via a severe heart attack. Kylie was stuck in seeing her life through the *High Achiever* perspective, so her body gave her the "shout" that something had to change.

Very rarely do we listen to the gentle whispers in life, so we have to hear an almighty roar! Kylie admitted that she would not have listened any other way so it needed to be given to her in this manner. We can get little niggles beforehand that something isn't right and that perhaps we have to change our lifestyle but our mind takes over and says it'll be fine, just another few years and then I can relax! Kylie realized that if she wanted to be around to see her children grow up, then she would need to make radical changes. This took a lot of courage on Kylie's part to make a career shift, but her body was demanding it. Slowly, slowly, her life came back into balance.

She started off with baby steps, bringing little pockets of joy into her life, as she claimed her creativity, did simple things, walked in nature, gave herself some stillness and reflective time. In other words, Kylie decided to be true to herself instead of feeding the belief system or archetypal pattern that said she must be successful, which is often gauged by how much money we make! This is a universally held belief, that our value is measured against how much money we have. One thing I can totally promise you is that this belief will not matter on your deathbed!

Kylie thought she had to play the *High Achiever* role to be approved of, but she learned it was not who she really was, but an Archetype that she had taken on board and made real because she put so much time into perfecting it. She had made it her truth by living it so profoundly that there was no other option but to give her this big shake up, so that change could be made.

This is how most of us operate, with the logical mind first and the heart last. It's not a great space to inhabit. I know that confused place well. Too many of us don't know what the word FEEL means, only the word THINK.

Sally came to see me to do some personal development work and the question arose regarding what she felt about something. Sally automatically answered from her mind, saying: I think this, this and this. But what do you feel Sally? She actually had no idea what she felt as she'd never gone within to find out. She confused thinking with feeling and thought they were the same thing.

This learned behavior came from her parents of course. No feelings were ever mentioned, they were not considered relevant or important, as only thinking was valid. This is not unusual. Does this apply to you too?

It sounds silly when I say that some of us have to learn how to feel, but if we don't know how to trust that part of ourselves, then we will automatically turn to over thinking to try and work out the answer. We will let our head rule over the heart's wisdom because we don't know how to do anything else (*Philosopher*).

This has been my experience too. One of the reasons I wasn't safe to feel and trust is because I grew up with an angry father, whom I was quite frightened of. It wasn't until I was on the metaphysical/spiritual journey that I came to understand I too had anger, but it was suppressed and denied.

My parents' denial about feelings (apart from my father's anger) dominated my childhood, teenage and early adult years. I had no idea I had emulated my parent's role modeling. I had no idea real joy existed. Or passion or heart expressed creativity. I've had to learn how to allow all these things into my life and thankfully grandchildren have helped me to soften into the joy. I so admire the parents who are able to freely allow their children to express their feelings without any judgments placed on good or bad behavior. Children like this learn that all feelings are valid and that there are safe and wise ways to express these feelings. This concept was totally foreign to my childhood where you were "seen and not heard!"

All I knew was to think logically and rationally and take on board what the education system, culture and the media of the day taught me. This is true for most of us, particularly my generation. Does this sound familiar?

OUR CONFUSING MINDS

Currently, on this planet, most of life is all about thinking rationally and logically. In the greater part of the world, we are a left-brain, dominant society. Please hear me clearly, we need to use our brain, it's part of the whole body system. Many wonderful discoveries would not have happened otherwise. However, the difficulty for most of us is that we **only** use our minds!

The truth is our hearts are just as important as our minds, and can guide us in the area of relationship, career, leisure time and so on. Science can now prove that the heart has its own brain and consciousness and in fact, what your heart feels guides the mind.

In regards to the wholeness of our brain, we forget the left-brain is only half of us. The other half, our right brain is where our creativity, our ingenuity, our spontaneity and intuition, plus all the fun, laughter and excitement we're capable of flows from. Our right brain is curious. It's drawn to the unusual, the unknown and the hidden parts of us. It's our secret weapon.

In our school years, when encouraged to go into the right brain to create something, it was usually attached to someone else's approval, like a teacher or parent. Then as we got older, it may have been the boss's approval that became important to us. True right brain creativity has no outcome. It is pure unfolding from the heart. Unfortunately we're not usually encouraged to come from this place.

Our mind, while a gift and an amazing tool, can bring us undone. It's that part of us that tells us we're not good enough. Our mind pushes us to strive harder regardless of whether we've anything more to give. Our inner critic sits in here, telling us we're worthless, shameful, guilty, or we'll never amount to anything!

It's this part of psychological mind that does a lot of damage, and unfortunately, the part we pay most attention to. It can be changed and bringing the right brain into balance with the left is a great place to start. Most of us don't understand that we're actually missing half of ourselves.

If this is you, don't despair, as there are a number of ways to learn how to open up to your right brain more, which will be discussed in a later chapter.

Margaret had a double PhD in two different subjects. She had been told about an Archetype Chart Reading and wanted to know a bit more about it. She came with expectations that her chart would be glowing with accolades about her intellectual achievements.

It was a shock to Margaret to find out that it actually said the opposite. Her mind was so powerful and strong and her belief was that it was the only thing that mattered in life. She played the *Perfectionist, Philosopher* and *Teacher* well. So well, that it actually took over her whole life as no other roles held any meaning for her.

But the chart said that there was no right brain activity going on at all. No emotion, no play, no laughter, no fun or no joy existed in her life. She was just striving for perfection and approval from others. Her body was trying to give her signals that said, "Look at the balance in your life."

But Margaret didn't want to hear this. She was completely disconnected from her body, her emotions, her feelings and intuition. It was almost akin to Margaret living constantly from the neck up, in her head. She held the belief that the body didn't really matter. It was only when it started to break down that it received any attention. Until that point, she took it for granted.

Margaret was not happy with the chart reading. All she wanted was to be told how wonderful she was because of her intellectual achievements but instead, the chart issued a warning that said pay attention or the body will give you a major wake up call. The charts will always give you the truth, but it doesn't mean to say you'll like it!

This way of living and thinking is all too common because of how the education system is structured, as well as expectations from parents or culture, so perhaps this applies to you?

However, I have great hope for the future, and that the old way of educating is slowly changing.

IS IT POSSIBLE TO CHANGE THIS AROUND?

If we want to live a fully empowered life, then we need to take control. We need to find a heart-based way of operating, to understand who is pulling at the levers when we have wobbly moments. This is where the Archetype work comes in.

It's a gift to be able to do an Archetype Chart for yourself, as it will show you whether your inner Child is operating from old fear based thoughts or if it's ready to become the Adult and step into it's fullest potential. However, this thought is scary for some of us. The fear of change keeps too many of us stuck.

You may ask, "But wouldn't I know if I was stuck?" The truth is, it's easier to see where other people are at, than ourselves. That's because we have an investment in the outcome. Our mind plays tricks with us. It might say, "Go on have that piece of chocolate cake because you deserve it." Then after you've had it, the same mind will give you the message that says, "You shouldn't have done that, where is your will power to resist?"

One day Charlotte came to see me; she was into total control of everything in her life. One could say almost to an extreme! An Archetype Chart was able to show her that her need to be in charge of everything came from her abusive background in her childhood. She had felt so out of control when she was a child that an inner part of her decided that the only way to stay safe, as the adult, was to control everything and everyone around her.

So Charlotte became the *Controller,* as sub-consciously, that was the role she believed she had to play to stay safe. For some of us, we block out our childhoods because they're so unpalatable, for others we learn how to control everything or to live in a fantasy world. This is how we escape a reality that was perhaps brutal, dangerous or emotionally damaging. It takes work to slowly change this around, little by little as we have to learn how to trust and feel safe to look at all of this. Gradually Charlotte was able to let go, to start trusting her intuition and heart's guidance, to find the balance between her left-brain and right-brain, and make other choices. I so admire Charlotte as she's found the courage to move forward and claim her own power back from a very degrading, shameful and damaging childhood.

This does not happen overnight of course, it can take years. But Charlotte truly wanted to be all that she could possibly be so that she felt empowered, in balance and able to start living life again, joyfully and happily.

Charlotte's story was a familiar one, where sexual abuse from a primary caregiver was prevalent. Of course she experienced total fear because she never felt safe. How could she? When we are not safe to be in our body, we have to turn elsewhere. Some of us will stay stuck in our head, as we're not safe to feel, shutting down the abusive experience and moving into denial.

Or perhaps we move to something else to make us feel good. We might turn our attention to how we look or what we achieve. Perhaps it's always giving to others, maybe getting lost in good causes, food, drugs, or other means of self-abuse. It can take many forms as we take on board different Archetypes to be noticed and loved such as the *Good Girl/Boy* or the *Lover*.

Charlotte had amazing courage as the adult to address all of this. She learned to go inside, to heal and comfort her inner child. Charlotte also found the courage to confront the abusive stepfather and move into a life of self-empowerment, choosing love not fear to guide her.

This won't be everyone's pathway, but it worked for Charlotte as she came to understand she was not the *Controller* but it was just a role she played to survive. Her inner child became Conscious enabling Charlotte to move into a more joyful and empowered life.

As you explore your Archetypes, you will begin to see familiar patterns emerging. You will see old beliefs coming to the surface so that you can deal with them and let them go.

Amy believed that she was unlovable and not worthwhile! She was often criticized as a child for not achieving enough, like her brother had. She was told that she should try harder or pay more attention. This criticism damaged Amy, so she started to withdraw. She felt misunderstood, not valued, not seen or heard. So Amy became the *Fantasy* Archetype as she daydreamed a lot. This played out with Amy not being present, always vague, not paying attention and listless. Amy also played out the *Escapist*, which meant that she would do anything she could to avoid the school system, do homework, or help around the house. The teachers often told her parents that Amy had the aptitude, but didn't put in enough effort! Of course, Amy felt like she didn't fit in, that she wasn't good enough and needless to say, always felt like she was being compared with her brother's high achievements. Perhaps this was your childhood experience too?

The chart showed Amy that the left-brain school system did not serve her, as she was predominantly right brain. The left-brain controls our thinking dominated behavior and the right brain brings forth our creativity and intuition. She was lethargic at school and could not be bothered with learning subjects that held no interest for her. As an adult, she just went from job to job, doing what she could to earn a living and pay the bills. But her heart was never in it.

The Chart showed her that her real passion lay in the right-brain and until she was expressing her true creativity, then her zest for life was lying dormant. We worked with ways to open up Amy's forgotten right brain, to bring it to life and find joy in living. Once Amy invested in herself and started expressing her creativity, everything in her life started to change.

The other side of this puzzle is the story about Clinton. He was excessively right brained, so totally creative and not in his body at all. He was constantly creating music, writing scores, painting or doodling. He had little common sense, found it hard to focus on anything outside of his music, forgot appointments, and even forgot to eat!

In fact, Clinton found it hard to communicate and be present with other people, often acting out as the *Clown/Fool*. This was a mask, as he did not feel comfortable in the outer world, just his inner world. Clinton's chart showed that he needed to develop his left-brain more and be coached in basic life skills so that he could function more easily in the world. His inner Child needed to grow up more and realize it was safe on the inner and outer levels. Wouldn't it be wonderful if we were taught all of this in the school system?

Another way to undermine ourselves is to have a *Bully* in our lives. John's chart showed him that his pattern was to attract in dominant personalities to overshadow him. He grew up with a very assertive mother, who tried to run his life up until the day she died. It was easier for John to simply give in and allow his mother her own way, than to fight for his independence. This pattern was strongly established in his childhood so he withdrew internally and just let his mother run his life. So it's no surprise that in his adult years, he kept on attracting in either dominant bosses or partners who also did the same thing.

John's task was to learn Assertiveness Training, so that he could confront the *Bully*, and stand in his own true power. Not from an anger perspective, but from an inner strength that said enough was enough! He had to build his self-worth and self-esteem so that he could do this, but his life changed forever once he found the courage to tackle this old, old issue.

John changed his attitudes and beliefs and therefore his whole demeanour altered. He no longer needed to attract in any *Bully* type protagonists any more. His mother no longer had power over him. He could be compassionate towards her as he could see where her need to control everything came from. John's mother did not like him taking his power back and becoming his own sovereign self. But John was as kind and caring as ever, just not acquiescent as he listened instead to his own inner wisdom. When someone presented with the old behavior, John no longer felt any fear or gave it any of his energy, so it simply disappeared from his life.

2

WHO ARE WE REALLY?

OUR EMOTIONS

Hopefully you can see that we're all made up of many different beliefs, attitudes and patterns and play out many different Archetypal roles to be approved of. So let's delve a little further. Most of us are very aware of our physical bodies but actually we have four bodies each working together at any one time and they're all interconnected.

You may want to throw the next part into one of your compartments marked Possible?

OUR EMOTIONAL BODY

A critical part of ourselves is our emotional or etheric body. This is where all our emotions are stored, such as fear or excitement. Sometimes you may feel frustration or anticipation. Maybe expectation. Feelings are generated from our emotions, they can be less intense but last much longer. For example, fear is an emotion but terror is a feeling.

Our feelings are governed by the maturity or evolvement of our inner child. Sometimes the child within just wants to have a huge temper tantrum. Other times, the child within expresses amazing wisdom and clarity. We can swing from one part to another. There are many books out there on emotional intelligence if you want to explore this further.

If your inner child is immature, then you will find yourself reacting to situations with anger, frustration, resentment, and fear, perhaps even denial! It may be that your inner child freezes or goes completely blank when an explosive situation occurs. This could be a violent situation at home, or a child being seriously ill. It could be your boss having a major meltdown or your partner or best friend walking out.

This happens because we're not safe to feel what's truly going on inside, so we use a fear based default setting that is familiar, like anger, numbness or frustration. We react to what's going on in an old way because we don't feel safe. All of us will experience this in one form or another.

A good example of this comes from my own childhood and growing up with an angry father who often exploded. My inner child would just freeze, not feel safe and therefore as an adult, I used to have the same reaction around anyone who expressed anger.

Eventually, I learned how to feel safe with anger and to stand my ground. I stopped taking it personally as I could see it for what it really is: the person expressing anger was playing out the child within, and having a temper tantrum because they're not getting their own way. It's a control weapon at the end of the day.

Mario had a mother who was very ill and had many trips to hospital whilst he was a youngster. He formed a mindset that said he wasn't safe because he never really knew if his mother would come home or not. This set up a pattern that said I can't trust life in precarious situations.

As the adult, when one of his own children became ill, he panicked and couldn't cope as his own inner childhood experiences came to the surface giving out fear based messages. He reacted unconsciously from this place. His fear based *Child* played out whenever he perceived things as dangerous. It wasn't the truth of course, but it was his knee jerk reaction to an old fear.

This then became a problem for his partner, his children and himself. He collapsed into the fear and let it control him as opposed to working with this old belief, and as the adult, seeing the illusion of it.

When the inner child has grown up, then you'll notice the feelings inside, but **choose** how to **respond** to the situation. You'll make a decision based on the intelligent mind working in union with the wise heart.

OUR MENTAL BODY

Next comes our mental body, which we all know about and probably all over use. Time and time again in chart readings, I see how dominant the mental body is, to the detriment of the other three bodies. The mental body stores your beliefs and programs that you've inherited, from your parents, culture, religion, education system, the media and your peer group.

From this comes your attitude to life and subsequently shapes what happens to you. It is fair to say that all of our pain and suffering comes from this body. *It's our beliefs that form our attitudes, that result in our emotions and feelings, that then give cause to what goes on in the physical realm.* This is a big statement, isn't it? Let me illustrate this a bit more.

Perhaps you've denied your own needs all your life, because you believe that you must serve others first and put your own needs last? I've found that this belief can produce various illnesses later on in life.

The thought that is fear based (*I'm only valid if I'm taking care of others*) can start in the mental body, move to the emotional body (*guilt if I say no to someone*) and end up manifesting in the physical body (ulcers, gut issues, lower back pain, reproductive organs and so on).

We are very multi-cultural in Australia so I often see women of a European background as clients. There is a strong mindset in these cultures that says family is of number one importance and you therefore become a *Slave* to your family's needs. Even if it costs you your own health to do so! This of course ties in really well with the *Martyr*. I've seen numerous women become seriously ill, as it's the only way they know how to say "I can't look after the grandchildren anymore!"

They fear speaking their truth, which is that they haven't got the energy to child mind any more: this is anathema to their culture. Then add the belief that they will be seen as "bad" grandmothers. It all results in things going downhill rapidly. So these women keep on going, even when it's obvious they have nothing left to give, because of the fear of what family and their peers will think of them.

How about the thought that says, "I can't trust anyone else to be there for me, (because of an abusive childhood) so I must always be in control and look out for myself." This comes from the mental body. It may translate into emotions of frustration and then feelings of anger if you don't get your own way, out of the desire to stay safe and in control. This may then lead to future physical symptoms of heart disease, adrenal collapse, or the central nervous system faltering, to name just a few.

We see this being played out with a lot of men in our culture. They were often not allowed to express any sensitive feelings, so they learned how to shut them down. As a consequence, they just use the left-brain rational, logical part of themselves or talk about "safe" subjects like sports, politics work and so on. They usually are not safe to talk about their feelings, their fears, hopes, dreams and wishes. They believe they are not safe to open up and share this vulnerable side of their nature.

It's a massive masculine mindset across the globe but thankfully, I see change happening with many young men these days who will make the paradigm shift that is necessary to bring us into harmony and peace from within.

OUR SPIRITUAL BODY

The last body is the spiritual body. This body remembers the truth of who you really are. It knows that you're really a *Being of Love*, that your true nature is love and is in fact, your true Essence. But again, we're not taught how to tune into this part of ourselves to access our own inner wisdom and guidance.

One way your spiritual body talks to you is via your intuition, but intuition sits in your right brain, and as we've already discussed this part of ourselves is often ignored and denied.

Thankfully, due to amazing technology, the energetic fields can be photographed and proven by Kirlian photography. So the four-body system is a valid entity but unfortunately not normally seen by ordinary, human eyes.

I share a common thought form with many that says our beliefs and attitudes create our biology. In other words, what you think or focus on, you create around yourself via your physical well-being, relationships and experiences.

If you believe you're hopeless and not good enough, then you will continuously attract in experiences that prove this to be the case. If you believe you're powerful and able to manifest well, then this too will be your experience and reality.

The Universe will always give you what you believe at the Unconscious and Subconscious levels. This is why the Sages throughout history have asked you to Know Thyself! When all four of your bodies are on the same page, then real magic begins to happen.

On many occasions I have been blessed to catch severe potential illness sitting in one of my other bodies. This gave me an opportunity to deal with the original cause or belief with regard to why it was there in the first place, so it didn't need to manifest as an illness. This is a blessing we can all learn, over time, but first we have to trust our intuition and let it guide us.

Sometimes my intuition guides me through dreams, sometimes I do a chart for myself to confirm the dreams. Other times I have a sense of "knowing" that something is wrong in my body.

My puberty years came on early. At ten I was developed. My sister and I heard the message constantly from our mother that our large bust size was a problem, as we couldn't get anything to fit us. So I grew up hearing that my body was a nuisance. Consequently I learned how to dislike my bust.

Perhaps thirty years later, I got a sense that illness was forming in my chest area. When I went inside to talk to this part of my body, I found that the resentment I was holding about my bust size had indeed formed pre cancerous cells that could manifest into a definite problem for me later down the track.

Unfortunately, at the level I'm talking about there's no instrument developed yet that can prove this to you, but I do have other friends with special gifts that can look into bodies and see what illness is lying there. Two friends of mine confirmed what I suspected, so I started the necessary work to heal these old thought forms.

I checked in with these same friends a few months down the track and the pre cancerous cells had disappeared. My intuition told me this, but sometimes the human part of us needs confirmation from elsewhere. I have discovered both personally and professionally, that resentment is one feeling that we do not have the luxury of hanging onto as it may cause severe illness further on in life.

I teach this work not only because it's a passion of mine, but also because I've lived it. There's an old saying: we teach what we most need to learn! I totally concur with that statement.

Your body is always trying to communicate with you. I was first pregnant at age twenty-three. My kidneys did not perform well and I became quite ill. At that time, I had no idea about the metaphysical/spiritual realms. So it wasn't until my late thirties that I came to understand why my kidneys stopped functioning. Kidneys are the seat of integrity in our body. They hold and process all of our fears. All my life I held a long-term belief that I wasn't safe to be here. This is not uncommon; I've come across it many times.

If this is your belief at the deepest level, then you'll create a situation to prove this to yourself. Hence my kidneys stopped working each time I was pregnant. Once I realized the falseness of this belief, I could then do something about it.

HOW ILLNESS CAN BE A GIFT

Usually the people who come to see me are confused, stuck, unhappy or very sick. People who want to get well but don't know how. This is the perfect moment to work on our archetypes. When we do an archetypal chart, it becomes obvious where and why we are stuck.

Over the years I've seen how almost all our illnesses stem back to our childhood programming, at the metaphysical level. Being told we need to be a certain way to be loved, valued, rewarded, safe, approved of, feted and encouraged to be what our parents think we should be.

Jack was a young man who was very ill. He was a motor mechanic. His father was from a European background and was thrilled to think his son would one day inherit his business and that his proud lineage would continue. The problem was that all Jack ever wanted to be was a hairdresser. Jack knew his father would radically disagree with this secret desire, so Jack had followed in his father's footsteps, just to please him.

Inside Jack felt resentment, anger, cheated and manipulated. Not surprisingly he became ill, very ill, and felt completely stuck to the point that he couldn't see the point in going on with his life, which was a tragedy as he was only in his twenties. This is the point where we connected, so we did an Archetype Chart Reading, which showed us how to deal with his issues.

Jack pulled Archetypes such as the *Worrier, Truth-Seeker* and *Trickster*. This chart asked Jack to look at his deepest fears. It challenged him to know his own truth and discover what tricks he was playing on himself.

So we set up some protocols to bring about change. Jack needed to learn how to honor and value his feelings; his self worth needed boosting, his inner strength and courage needed to come out. There are many techniques that teach you how to do this, and I cover some of them at the back of this book.

Jack was still ill of course, but eventually his father dropped all his expectations and actually asked him what would it take for him to get better? The truth finally came out and Jack's father agreed that Jack should leave the business to pursue his dream. Jack's father finally realized that his beliefs about what Jack should be doing were getting in the way of Jack's healing. His love for Jack won the day. Jack didn't need his illness anymore, as he was finally living from his own truth.

It's amazing how we can use illness as a pathway to freedom, in an effort to shift out of an unbearable situation. We usually don't know this at the time, it often only becomes clearer down the track.

Some use ill health to manipulate others, to get attention, to feel loved and valued, but at a huge cost. When Lily came to see me she had multiple sclerosis, which was totally debilitating and life threatening. When I 'scanned' Lily's body and did an archetype reading on her, it became obvious that Lily had a strong interest in remaining ill (*Actor and Villain Crook*).

Her multiple sclerosis guaranteed her lots of attention, even though she paid a big price for this attention. Lily was taking on board the sick role because it had a pay off and guaranteed that all her needs were met. She got to blame everything that happened in her life on the MS. The *Villain Crook* Archetype almost demands a serious question: "How am I ripping someone else off or what am I doing to rip myself off?"

When I raised this question with Lily, about using illness to meet her needs and therefore ripping herself off from living a full and healthy life, she agreed. I explained there was no point in us getting together as she actually didn't want to get better. Please hear me clearly - I am not suggesting for one minute that this is true of anyone with a serious illness; I am just saying that this was true in this particular instance. Lily agreed with me that there was a payoff happening here.

Learning more of Lily's story I discovered that Lily had felt abandoned as a child. She had gone through Second World War experiences and had to escape to another country. So illness became her way of getting attention. Lily went on to say, "You'll only hear me say these words in this room - I will completely disown them outside of this room!"

It's shocking to hear of someone who really wants to be so ill, but most of us are imprisoned with beliefs that don't serve us often because of trauma. The question is whether we want to be like Jack and take the leap, or to stay stuck like Lily.

If you want to push forward then you need to get to know your current values, to become aware of the crippling beliefs you've inherited from your cultural background, the education system or religion.

Teresa was from a Catholic/Italian background. Family was everything. In an ideal world, you married and produced lots of grandchildren. The dilemma was that Teresa was actually gay and her parents did not know this. She pretended to go out with men and brought them home occasionally. Her mother was constantly asking her when she was going to get married and have children.

I saw Teresa at a time when she had huge gut issues. Nothing seemed to be helping her and she believed she'd tried everything. The Archetypes that Teresa pulled challenged her, such as the *Square Peg in a Round Hole, Coward* and *Fool's Love.* The chart showed that her gut issues were actually coming from her emotional body, as she was literally living a lie and hiding her true nature, which was making her sick. Her gut was saying "I can't stomach this any longer!"

The *Square Peg in a Round Hole* Archetype means that we feel different to everyone else, we feel like we don't belong and for some, it even means apologizing for everything that you do. This is explained in more detail later on, but suffice to say this is how Teresa felt. So, like most of us, Teresa had to choose between being true to herself (and owning her sexuality) or pretending to be who she wasn't, to keep her parents happy.

Fortunately Teresa had the courage to be honest and open with her parents, help her fearful inner child become Conscious, risk their disapproval and get on with her life. The good news is that her parents grew into acceptance of this once they got over their initial shock.

What unhelpful beliefs are you carrying from your parents, from your family of origin or adopted parents? This question takes courage to answer.

OTHER IMPOSED BELIEFS

There are many ways we can fool ourselves. Ken looked like he had a successful life. But the Archetypal Chart showed otherwise. There was a strong *Saboteur* playing out in his life. He was abused as a child and made to work long hours on his parent's property. His father physically tormented him repeatedly, as did his mother. At sixteen, he left his parent's home and moved to the city.

His childhood left a lot of emotional scars, which he tried to hide with working hard, cracking jokes, pretending everything was fine, as well as helping others. He was desperate for the attention of people who could restore his faith that not everyone was like his parents.

He struggled to survive, worked hard and eventually carved out a career for himself. Financially, he did well. But his core belief was around struggle. This manifested in how hard his life was, the person he eventually married and the different scenarios that played out which showed him that he still couldn't trust anyone to guide or help him! He had to do it all on his own or else he would be betrayed somehow or other. He kept on repeating his childhood experience, but in an adult manner.

His inner Child was still calling the shots. Ken didn't really trust anyone, males or females, so he was often lonely and isolated. It took some work to help him see these beliefs were coming from within, then realize he could change them and therefore create a different reality in his outside world. It was a while before he truly understood that what he felt and believed created his external experiences. Slowly, slowly, he learned how to trust in himself and others, but it can be the work of a lifetime.

The Universe or Life will always give us what we believe to be true. The trouble is, we're not in touch with our deepest truth. What we think at the conscious level is not necessarily true at the unconscious and sub-conscious level and it's from this place that we create our life experiences.

In other words, if what we thought in our conscious mind really were true, then all of us would lead brilliant lives, full of abundance across the board. So for Ken, it meant that things did go wrong because he was invested heavily in his old thoughts of struggle, pain and suffering. But through his desire to change, he started turning all of this around.

Though it might cause a little discomfort, we need to look at our religion also and see how certain beliefs we've grown up with may not be serving us.

There are many different religions, ideologies, dogma and fundamentalists on the planet today. The love, caring and sharing that can come from some of these groups can be life sustaining. However, there are also fear based beliefs that are indoctrinated from an early age that I see do a lot of damage to some adults. One such belief is guilt. This belief is used to control people. It is an insidious feeling that serves no purpose whatsoever. However, genuine remorse can be most necessary for true healing to occur.

Over the years, I've come across many women, (usually from a Christian background) who take on board a belief that they're unworthy, the *Disciple* Archetype. They are consumed by guilt because the Minister or Priest has told them that they're sinners. In fact, children are still taught today that they are sinners. The fear is they won't be considered pure enough to get through the Pearly Gates and instead will go to Hell. These are beliefs or interpretations that they've been given or inherited, usually from the Old Testament version of God.

My answer is to sack that God and get a new one because the God they believe in is vengeful, judgemental and unloving. I work with clients through their guilt and worthiness issues, showing them that it's a belief that they have taken on board from their religion, but it's not the truth of who they are. The concept of sin is used as a control mechanism.

It needs to be examined and really felt into, so that your own heart can give you the truth, not doctrines handed down through the ages.

What about your peer group? How have they influenced you to fit in, become accepted, as well as liked and approved of? Maybe it's getting your hair cut in a certain way, or dressing to get a particular look, perhaps speaking a language that is considered cool? It could be giving your power away sexually because all your friends are doing so! Perhaps dangerously vandalizing other people's property because it's considered outrageous but also fun!

There are so many ways we try to fit in, because of our fear of being left out, isolated or alone. In fact, there is a term now called F.O.M.O. or the Fear Of Missing Out. This is exacerbated by Social Media in a big way. Now there are professionals who just deal with bullying by Social Media: and the pressures that come with being online and comparing yourself to your peer group.

It can focus on how many friends we have, are we having a fun time and doing exciting new things? If not, then there's something wrong with us! These are all imposed beliefs and simply not true, but we latch onto them, give them our energy and therefore make them true. No wonder depression is now the number one illness in the world and the suicide rate amongst young people is growing.

Bullying has become very dominant, particularly in schools. No doubt it's always been there, but it seems to be much worse or perhaps more publicized. This publicity is a good thing as bullying is cruel, isolating and destructive and needs to change. Behind the need to bully someone, there's usually a lost soul desperate for love.

Which leads me to the education we received. What messages did you take on board at school? Did you believe the teacher who told you that you were a failure and would never amount to anything? What about the teacher who told you to stop doing art or singing classes because they're not for you as you weren't good enough?

How much pressure did you feel from the school, as well as your parents, to achieve great results? Did you get the message that if you didn't get first class results, then somehow you're a disappointment and therefore not lovable or worthwhile? So many young people become depressed, anxious and have panic attacks because they believe they're not enough in some way. Where do these beliefs originate?

We are so impressionable in our childhood and teenage years. We believe our scholastic results define us. This is what we are taught. However, we are so much more than this.

One day we may have a mainstream education system that is holistic, integrating left brain and right brain. Hopefully it will take on board your emotional body, teaching us how to go within. We will learn how to trust in our own discernment process, evaluating with our hearts as well as our brains.

For so many of us, we've only been validated for what we think. We've been taught that our negative emotions like anger, sadness, disappointment and so on have to be solved immediately, changed and moved into positive emotions. We are shamed if we feel like this. One day all our emotions will be validated and the label of good/bad or right/wrong will be eliminated.

And what about the media? Are you a sucker for "reality" television shows? *The Bachelor? Cooking shows? Survivor,* or *Married At First Sight?* How do they influence who you are and how you operate in the world? Have you ever examined the messages behind the sitcoms and talk shows? Perhaps you just take them on board as gospel truths because that's what the media or Society tell you to do?

Do you have to watch three news services a night in case you miss something? Do you believe that what you see on television, or read in the newspapers, is the truth? Where does this come from?

Advertising is a huge billion-dollar industry and much research has been conducted around how to sell things to vulnerable minds in prime time. Do you vicariously live through "reality" type shows as it means you don't have to therefore go out and create a life for yourself?

When we're ready, usually through the catalyst of a crisis or upheaval of some sort, we start to dig a little deeper to get to our core truth. This may seem like hard work to some, but it usually pays off. Often I find from the archetype readings that the background you've had is perfect for your growth. All the difficulties, all the knotty problems can act as a springboard to catapult you into a new way of being and behaving.

As already mentioned, my parents were very mind based. My father was well educated and very opinionated about everything that was happening around him. Looking back I can see he had a strong *Philosopher* at his Unconscious level, which meant he would give his opinions to all and sundry. He had a huge need to be heard and validated. He was addicted to being right and came across as the authoritarian figure. Challenging him was tricky.

My mother was the quintessential *Good Girl*; she never rebelled or rocked the boat. However, many years down the track, I discovered that while my father was an overt *Controller*, my mother was the covert *Controller*. My father's anger was visible and experienced by us all. My mother however, was a subtle manipulator who got her own way eventually, but in a surreptitious manner.

The bottom line is that we're actually all *Controllers* in some way or another, but the way this is expressed is varied. It may be how you like to stack the dishwasher, or have your cupboards look just right. Maybe it's how you store things on your computer, or have things organised on your bed, or in your workshop, but all of us have controlling tendencies.

So how do we grow up and drop old, fear-based beliefs?

3

DECIDING TO GROW UP

It was living under such a controlled manner that pushed me towards understanding why we do what we do. Eventually I came to see that my parents were perfect for my growth. Having zero emotional input in my life forced me to go and seek it elsewhere. Apart from intimate relationships, I found it in the spiritual/personal growth pathway by understanding my motivations behind actions and exploring the many avenues to love.

I have said numerous times that if I didn't have a twin sister, then I doubt I would have survived the journey as we tend to either emulate our parents' patterning or go in the opposite direction. Changing behaviors and patterning can be a very isolating journey, and may even feel like the "dark night of the soul" sometimes. But this is the test – do we have the courage to be true to ourselves?

Or will we keep on doing same old, same old by not rocking the boat and therefore denying our soul's truth of who we really are? Only our hearts can give us this deepest truth.

What does your heart tell you?

THE ENERGY OF JUDGMENT

Nearly all of us grow up with a strong inner *Judge*, which usually means hearing judgment of some sort all the time. This criticism can be personal or global. We need to understand that the only reason we use judgment is to feel superior or inferior to another, so that we can buy into better than or less than.

We are taught judgment from the moment of our birth. Perhaps it's with regard to how cute we are, how well do we do at school, are we fitting the desired latest trend as a teenager, or what job do we have as an adult. When you judge another, it's often saying, "you're wrong and I'm right." When this happens, we often get to feel superior and righteous. You judge from the mind. In effect what we're doing is isolating ourselves, by separating out from our true nature of the heart.

The funny thing is that our mind does not know the difference between a lie and the truth. It only knows what you feed it. It has no idea that this judgment, spoken or unspoken, about yourself or another, is going within and sits in the body at a cellular level.

Metaphysically speaking, one illness that may derive from judgment (of others or the self) is arthritis, in its various forms. It may be akin to hot anger (judgment) stored in the joints. A lifetime of judgments passed about self or others can mean serious health issues as we age. We may find ourselves with a heart or lung condition, throat problems or mental health issues, maybe hip or leg difficulties.

These may unfold because judgment is a mental process. This means you're using your mind all the time to feel superior or inferior. The heart does not get a look in. So if your heart wants to give you a strong message that you're ignoring it, or out of balance, then illness may be created in that area, such as heart or lung issues arising.

Our throat center can represent the seat of our Will, so by constantly judging ourselves or others, spoken or unspoken, then we're making a statement that says ignore the heart's truth and just keep on doing judgment because it's acceptable. So again, our mind is very powerful and the heart gets pushed aside. Our bodies are always trying to speak to us about where our belief systems sit.

This may be a whole new concept for you to think about and feel into around the energy of judgment. It's automatic for nearly all of us as we just accept it as the norm and do it because everyone else does it.

It helps when we can recognize that we all have judgment in us. I've been extremely judgmental at times. Sometimes towards myself, when I've done things that are not in integrity, but mostly towards others, though it was usually unspoken. It took me quite a few Archetype charts to understand what I was doing to myself. Every time my mind would pass unspoken judgment on another, it separated me out from my heart.

These days I can catch myself exercising judgment. I see it for what it is, a trick of my mind, and therefore I choose to let go of the judgment. I open up instead to the understanding that I have no right to judge, as I am not walking in that person's shoes. This is what it takes to grow up. Sadly our inability to deal with our lack of self worth, which prompts us to be judgmental in the first place, brings us down.

If there were one thing I'd love to get rid of in life it's judgment, as it's such a destructive way to live. We judge without thinking or realizing what we're actually doing. We accept it as the norm because everyone does it, person-to-person, country-to-country, religion-to-religion and so forth.

What we need to develop instead is **discernment**, which is a necessary quality to imbue as we move through life. Let me give an example to explain the difference.

Suppose you're walking through a park and you see a badly made bench that's about to collapse. Discernment says that's a badly made bench. Judgement says, that's a badly made bench and the person who made it shouldn't ever be allowed to make another! One observes, the other criticizes. The truth is, we have no idea how the bench came to be badly made or how it got to that condition. But we feel it's our right to always judge things and situations. Discernment has no impact on the body, but judgments, over time, can cause many problems.

Whom do you judge? Yourself? Perhaps others? Why?

MOVING ON

Of course there are reasons behind all our unhelpful behaviors, such as poor self image, self worth or no self love.

Most of us do not have good role models to encourage us to turn these behaviors around. As we start to peel back the layers of our vulnerable selves, we need to be kind and patient, knowing that we have the resources to come into deeper awareness and therefore kindness to ourselves.

Sometimes it feels like an impossibly high mountain to climb, shedding layer after layer. But there's no rush, take little steps, greet each day as it comes, be present in the moment, and trust in the unfolding.

Perhaps your little steps look like giving yourself fifteen minutes a day to be quiet and still, simply gazing out a window, emptying busy mind and just BEING. We are so good at playing Human Doings, rather than Human Beings! Maybe it's joining a yoga class, doing Pilates or even belly dancing! Perhaps you need to go horse riding once a week or go out on your motorbike to clear out cobwebs? How about swimming?

What is that you can do for yourself that makes your heart sing or lifts you up, energetically speaking? Don't wait, just do it.

Sometimes it's the innocuous things in life, like vacuuming the house, that bring about light bulb moments. I remember thinking: *There has to be more to life than being someone's wife, someone's mother, someone's daughter, someone's sibling or doing a job?* It's funny how some of our greatest breakthroughs come in seemingly mundane ways.

At that pivotal point in my life I literally felt bolts of energy go through me. At last change was afoot, but I wasn't consciously aware of it at the time. In those days I was not in touch with my feelings, how I was living and what I was doing.

Have you experienced these light bulb moments?

Innocuous moments can later prove to be huge catalysts for change. The Archetype Chart readings online only came about because a friend yelled at me one day asking when was I going to get real and join the digital age? My bodily response was huge and lasted for about thirty minutes. I knew she had just opened up a major doorway for me to walk through, even though it felt very daunting financially and professionally.

One other time I was doing a meditation and I heard the message loud and clear that said I was to walk the Magdalene trail in the south of France. I have learned not to dismiss anything, just allow it to open up and unfold.

Within two weeks, not only did workshops unfold to give me the money to do this, but also a good friend paid for my airline tickets. I was even sent Business Class! Experience shows me that when I follow these strong intuitive flashes, huge learning curves unfold that help me to remember more and more the efficacy of my own true nature.

If I'd had a loving upbringing, then maybe I would never have asked that pivotal question. So whatever your present and past life circumstances, trust they are and have been perfectly right for you to learn and grow into the extraordinary human being you are, beneath all your confusion and uncertainty.

Some of us get the message to move on easier than others. Often it does take a crisis to make the required changes. Rarely do we make necessary change when we're coping, feeling in charge and everything is going just how we want it to go. We love being in our comfort zones and do not step out of them willingly.

Don't beat yourself up if the "hard road" is how life has been for you, just know if you do the work then the possibility of everything changing for you is greatly enhanced. A few weeks, a few months, a year on you may very well not recognize your present self, as your new wiser, more empowered self emerges.

One of my teachers Stephen Levine used to say, "Pain becomes its own reward." By that he meant only when we've had enough of the pain, no matter what it is or how it manifests, do we move on. Eckhart Tolle, a well known Spiritual Teacher, calls it the Pain Body. Until we reach that point of "enough" we keep going round and round in circles, repeating the same lessons over and over again. I've done this many times at different points in my life. I often say I have a PhD in two steps forward and ten steps back!

SEEKING APPROVAL

Maybe there was a part of you looking for your parents' approval? If so, how did this play out for you? Perhaps by trying to please them, placate them or be what they wanted you to be? Maybe it's still happening?

When we constantly seek outside approval, it simply means we're not yet capable of trusting ourselves. We stay the child, wanting an external authority figure to approve of us. This theme comes up in the Charts over and over again.

I've met clients in their forties, fifties and sixties who still seek their parent's approval for every decision that is made, whether the parent is in the physical body or not, or even in the same country! All their decisions are run past the adage: would my parent or parents approve of me doing this? Mostly this is unconscious behaviour and is called co-dependency.

Whose approval do you need before you can make a decision? In what area of your life does this play out?

What I love about the archetypes is how powerfully they can move us on, propelling us beyond old habits and patterns that no longer serve us. It's a joyous thing to see others move on from a debilitating situation.

Perhaps you grew up with your *Victim* Archetype believing life was too hard, everyone else was to blame for your circumstances and that you had no idea how to shift the situation? Sometimes we can get so stuck as deep down we can't imagine how else life can be, believing we're a lost cause. But there's no such thing in this Universe.

So it's totally uplifting to see someone take their power back from the *Victim* of the past and move it to a higher level where their life flows with ease and grace because they have shifted old beliefs, attitudes and values.

There's nothing that will be shared here that you don't already know deep within your being. Whether or not you access your inner wisdom depends on how honest you are with yourself. The charts can be affirming, confirming or maybe a foot up the backside.

The question is whether or not you're ready to own these insights? Your Archetypes are like reading a life script, but it's up to you how you play out your script. So you can wake up to empowerment or stay stuck in a disastrous script.

FEAR OF CHANGE

I've had clients who have been stuck in relationships that are finished or destructive, but their fear of change keeps them there. At times, as we progress, you may feel strong fear arising around the potential changes that need to be made. If so, don't shy away from this fear. Journey to the heart of this fear, face it, and you will see how this fear has long imprisoned you and those close to you.

Remember the acronym for F.E.A.R - False Evidence Appearing Real. Know whatever is for your highest good, is automatically for the highest good of those around you, even if it means leaving your job or your relationship.

Perhaps it's choosing to move on from a toxic family situation. Others may not make this connection like you do, but over time this will prove to be the wisest pathway.

In an abusive relationship, some choose the *Coward*, preferring to pretend there isn't a problem. They hope that it will simply go away or else justification comes in to explain why they stay in a toxic pattern.

In some cases, it does not surprise me when I see them again, to find out that their partner has been having an affair. Sometimes it takes quite some effort for them to see that at the unconscious level they've had a part in making the affair happen! They couldn't find the courage to walk away, so the Universe stepped in and did it for them. The Archetypes will show you this in the chart reading.

This is not true for everyone obviously. Some of us embrace change with ease, finding it exciting to move jobs because they love the challenge of testing themselves in a new field. Others have the courage to move half way around the world to begin a new life. But some of us have enormous difficulty in moving from one suburb to another, changing schools, or driving out of our local district.

We're all uniquely different, so what one person finds easy to accomplish, another person can find extremely difficult. We're all at different stages of our growth and awakening.

Some Archetype Charts show me that a person is ready to finish off a major section of their life's journey, but it can also mean that they're ready to start a new phase. This often involves going right back to the beginning again.

It's like being a big fish in a little pond at primary school, then you move to secondary school and go right back to the beginning, a small fish in a big pond. That's a metaphor for life really. It's helpful to understand this journey through the chart's perspective.

For me, life is like an enormous stage and we invite different characters to play out on our stage. No matter who appears on your stage, there's something to be learned from each one of them.

Some people are here to teach us humility, others how to stand up for ourselves. Others are just here for love and support. Some are here to challenge us to be our true magnificence instead of settling for a mediocre life. We all have so many different characters coming and going on the stage of life.

It's not what these characters are doing to you that is the issue; it's how you react and respond to them that makes life so interesting and where the real wisdom lies. At the end of the day, we're all doing the best job we know how, so compassion for the self is paramount.

WHAT WE CAN'T SEE!

Wisdom often only comes in hindsight. At the time of upheaval life can feel like a disaster. Sometimes the changes we need to make are subtle, but even this can feel like a big ask. This is when we may be tempted to fall into the *Drama Queen* or the *Victim*.

Caroline learned from a very early age that any attention is better than none, even negative attention. So everything became a drama for her. If she didn't do well in a test at school, then the world was about to end. As she grew up, if she didn't have the best looking boyfriend, then life was horrible and it wasn't fair. This became the lens with which she viewed the world. If it didn't suit her or fit her map of the world, then it was awful and life was not fair.

In time, Caroline had three children. However, no one was as tired as she was. No one had more problems with her children than she did and everything in her life was about drama and one upmanship. It was an addictive behavioral pattern that she had no idea she was running. The problem is that when you're in it, you can't see it! Because this was Caroline's belief system about life being unfair, then this is what she kept on bringing to herself. She didn't understand that it was self perpetuating.

It took quite a bit of work for Caroline to see what she was doing to herself and her family. She could easily see the *Drama Queen* in others, but not in herself. When *Drama Queen* is playing out at the Unconscious level, then you either create drama in your own life (often continuously), or borrow someone else's to feel involved, to feel important, or to be noticed. She had no idea she was being a *Victim* either. This is the "poor me" aspect, the part within us all that feels the need to blame others for where life has taken us. Caroline constantly reinforced everything that was wrong, very rarely did she show appreciation for what was right. This was a way of living for Caroline, constantly feeling sorry for herself and not able to get out of the hole that had she had unknowingly dug for herself. It never occurred to Caroline that her beliefs were reinforcing the outcome all the time.

Thankfully, the charts kept bringing this to the surface. What was required was an attitudinal shift of perspective, along with acceptance and gratitude. Caroline was headed for illness to learn this lesson, but thankfully she caught it before it needed to manifest in her body. We all get to make choices, especially if it's an inside job about our attitude to life.

It's sometimes very hard to see these Archetypes playing out when you're in the middle of the drama. We all play so many different roles; we unknowingly pull in different Archetypal patterns to get attention or to stay safe. Hopefully your Higher Self steps in at the right time to give you the gift of awareness so that we can wake up and make different choices. Or maybe an "angel" appears in the guise of another human being that can point you in another direction, lovingly and without judgment?

Have you been the *Drama Queen?* Most teenage girls play this role at some point. It's exhausting being around the drama, whether it's playing out in the home, at work, on the sporting field or maybe Facebook!

Behind all of the roles we play, we are all only yearning for acceptance, love, the feeling of belonging and being safe to be our authentic selves. Because of these innate desires we take on board various roles or Archetypes hoping that they will give us the happiness we desire.

Some cultures define happiness by what you achieve via your academic qualifications, while other cultures define happiness by how much money you have. Yet happiness is an inside job. No person or job can make you happy. You can only decide to BE happy

As you get to know yourself and where you are at, it helps to remember we were born as *Love,* but raised in fear based beliefs. Our task is to re-member, to go back home to *Love,* to our true Nature. Our heart is our foundation. Moving from the head to the wisdom of the heart is the greatest journey you will ever take.

As the spiritual teacher Mooji says, we're all suffering from a case of mistaken identity. We believe we are our achievements.

We believe we're the body/mind connection. We believe we're our assets. Yet none of this matters when you're dying! It's not who you are, it's what your experience has been, that matters. But we mistake experience with the truth of who we are. Where are we taught this valuable information?

The journey from the mind to the heart is physically the shortest journey, but often seen as scary because of the fear of the unknown: what will you discover or what will you have to give up? However, at the deepest level of your Being, it's not unknown at all. It's who you really are. Are you ready to take the first few powerful steps?

4

THE UNCONSCIOUS LEVEL - TRIBAL

Some scholars talk about four different levels of Consciousness: Unconscious, Subconscious, Conscious and Super Conscious.

The Unconscious level, which may also be referred to as the Tribal or hidden level means that we're not aware of why we do the things we do. We mostly accept what we've been taught by our parents, teachers, religion or culture and continue without any real understanding behind our actions. We tend to do things out of automaticity, and without question.

We all start off at this Tribal level as it represents the Outer Persona we project to the world. Another way of saying this could be that it is the image we give out and how we portray ourselves. For most of the time, we have no genuine idea why we're doing what we're doing as most things are done simply because this is what we've been taught.

Have you ever thought of this conundrum? It simply doesn't occur to us to examine our motivations with regard to why our life plays out like it does.

This is because no one asks us to look deeply within; it's all about looking outwards at the physical world. We accept this because we are not taught anything else. Things are just the way they are and we're expected to follow suit. Unless you were into rebellion as a child or teenager, (*Rebel*) you simply conformed, to stay safe, to be approved of and to be loved.

The Tribe commands strong adherence to its beliefs and culture and one simply accepts it is true because the culture says it's true.

We have quite a large Indian population here in Melbourne, Australia, and I remember seeing a young Indian man, Sanjeev, who had fallen in love with an Australian girl. His parents were mortified as they expected to choose this young man's bride. It was the accepted reality where they came from and their tribal beliefs were challenged to the hilt when Sanjeev told them of his plans to become engaged to this young woman. To his parents, this was outrageous and totally against their culture, but to Sanjeev who was half Australian, it was the way his peer group behaved and therefore the norm.

Australia, like many other countries, is extremely multi cultural. Sometimes these different values, expectations and beliefs create uncomfortable situations as cultures clash, ignorance prevails and rigid viewpoints are adhered to.

In today's world, most teenagers in Australia have a mobile phone. It is considered strange if you didn't have one. It's necessary to check for messages from friends, what's happening on social media, to be contactable all the time as well as know what's going on at the weekend! You will have a mobile if you want to feel accepted, and want to fit in. To not have one would imply that you're different, that you're weird and not part of the Tribe. We all long to be accepted, we want to belong, and to feel part of something that supports and nurtures us.

Does your family or culture have certain beliefs that dictate your choices? Are you sometimes caught between cultures or peers and their expectations?

Recently, I also saw this playing out in Bali. One beautiful, young woman had to follow in a certain cultural and shamanic lineage, though her heart wanted her to do something else. She became quite ill when she wouldn't follow in this lineage, in fact, she came very close to dying. Eventually her parents begged her to go back to her heritage or else she would die. To please her parents and to save her life, she agreed. This choice gave her back her life, but at what cost?

When I saw her, even though she was excellent at what she did, her heart appeared to be elsewhere. It felt like she was operating out of automaticity, rather than coming from joy. She had clearly made a choice that was right for her culture. The authority of the tribe was very present and strong. This is the epitome of what the Tribe, Clan, Group or Nation can command. But at a personal level, was it right for her? Who knows?

OUR PHYSICAL BODIES

When you're setting off in life you're taught you are just your Physical body, therefore you only have the five senses of taste, sound, sight, touch and smell. The tangible outside world is all there is. So if something goes wrong in your life, it's only due to your physicality.

Fiona had been diagnosed with breast cancer and had followed the traditional recommended treatments of surgery and then radiation. She felt good once the treatment was over and just got on with her life. About three years later, the cancer returned but this time to the lungs. We looked at other reasons as to why this would happen, instead of just pursuing the medical model.

I find this in many cases, where traditional medical treatments are applied to severe illnesses, because the belief is you're only the physical body. Often the illness returns, at a later stage, but sometimes in another place. Have you noticed this too?

This appears to be the experience of the majority of people, particularly in the west, because we're locked into a certain way of thinking. Many people give their power away to the medical model. If you have a life threatening disease and the doctor tells you that your life expectancy is two years, then that's usually exactly what you'll have. We believe the doctors know more than us and in many ways they do, but it never occurs to us, at this level, to do our own research or find another way of dealing with things.

As Dr. Deepak Chopra says, "Believe the diagnosis but not the prognosis!"

Because of her chart reading, Fiona came to see that she had never had any self love, self nurturing or self worth. Fiona had the *Slave* and *Rescuer* Archetypes in her chart. At the core of her Being, she believed she always had to give to others to stay safe. Fiona often was a slave to other people's needs, usually at the cost of denying her own. She was also addicted to rescuing others, fixing them, helping them, again often at a cost to herself. This is what boosted her self worth and helped Fiona to feel good about herself as she saw them getting stronger and moving on with their lives. But she paid a high price for these actions with her health. Fiona had to dig deep to find out if the price she paid was worth it. So we worked together to start the healing process.

I believe there is room for many ways of handling different issues that arise in the physical body and the medical model is just one of them. It's a brilliant model and I've been grateful for it many times over. It has given life and hope to many, but it's not the only one.

The technology that is around now is awe inspiring, but there are many other maps of the world if we only bother to explore them. Dr. Bruce Lipton's Epigenetics model is an excellent example.

Dr. Lipton explains that our genes, our DNA, accounts for a small percentage of who we actually are. It was the old scientific belief that said our DNA was responsible for so much of what happened to our bodies and our life experiences. Dr. Lipton discovered that it's our environment that shapes our reality and influences us much more than our genes. Things like our culture, our beliefs, our religion, the food we eat, or how stressful our lives are, play a huge role. This means we can no longer blame our lives on the genes we inherited. Dr. Lipton's book, *The Biology of Belief* explains his research thoroughly.

If we believe that we're just our body, then it's a shock if very fit people just drop dead of a heart attack. According to the Tribe, it's inconceivable how this could happen because they were so healthy and exercised a lot. However, when this has happened to people I've known and I've looked at their energy field, their emotional and mental system was suppressed, repressed and often depressed.

I hope this makes sense to you. It's hard to think outside the square if we've never been given the opportunity to do so, or we're told it's wrong or rubbish.

DO AUTHORITY FIGURES PRESS YOUR BUTTONS?

Being Unconscious means we give our power away to other authority figures, such as parents, teachers, religion, bosses or maybe even wealthy people. Indeed anyone who has any level of authority over us. It may also be those whom we wish to impress. **Fear,** under the guise of panic or anxiety, usually arises when the possibility of challenging these authority figures comes up. What happens to you? Do you feel clammy, sick to the stomach or perhaps your throat closes over and you can't speak?

Craig came to see me after he'd been wiped out financially. It's not fun when you have to deal with the Taxation Office because of perceived misappropriation of funds. It overwhelmed him as they represented a huge Authority figure to Craig. When we're still unconscious, the panic that comes over the body feels all consuming. This is because we have no inner authority, it is all placed outside of ourselves, so it's very hard to calm down and see another viewpoint.

We were able to work together to move through his fears and to help him see a bigger picture of why this happened to him. Craig had pulled the *Midas* Archetype and it was easy for him to see that he'd inherited old belief systems from his father and culture, around money, that did not serve him. He believed that life was a struggle: his father had shown how to live in the future, always thinking that the next big job would be the one to make him millions of dollars. He never experienced a male role model that showed him how to handle money wisely. So he just kept on perpetuating the patterns that he'd learned from his father. So the wake up call from the Taxation Office was really an opportunity to change an old pattern. Fortunately Craig could see it this way too. Do you know someone like this?

In this Unconscious field, you are stuck in duality, meaning you believe in opposites. Opposing beliefs such as good and bad, or right and wrong, perhaps heaven and earth, or wealth versus poverty. If someone has done something to you, then you have to have revenge and pay him or her back.

No doubt this sounds very familiar when you look at our planet and see the many wars that are operating. If someone has betrayed you, then you have to hurt him or her back. Can you relate to this feeling? Has it happened to you?

At one point, Deborah came into my life. Her father left her when she was young and never had any future contact with her. Like most little girls, all she wanted was to see her dad, so she waited and waited for him to get in touch, but this never happened. Her sadness and feelings of rejection were huge. He was the ultimate authority figure who was not available to her. This set up a core belief that she was unlovable and couldn't trust any males to be there for her. So the energy of betrayal sat strongly with her.

Move forward to Deborah's adult years when her lover betrayed her, which of course devastated her. Deborah just wanted to get back at him because he wiped out her future plans of marriage and a family, in fact her dream of happy ever after! Deborah had the *Mother/Father* in her chart as well as the *Healer*. The Chart was telling her it was time to deal with her Father issues and heal old wounds.

With time and help, Deborah could eventually understand how her childhood beliefs played a part in this relationship. All her adult intimate relationships were unsatisfactory and hurtful because she couldn't and wouldn't let love in. Her beliefs were telling her she was not safe to be vulnerable and to open up to experience love. She had "closed" her heart down to love, yet it was the thing she craved the most, as we all do. How familiar is this story? Deborah eventually learned how to bring in a new way of relating to self and to others.

Politics sit in this Tribal or Unconscious realm. When you're a big player, on a global stage, then the scenario of, "I am more powerful than you and I'll prove it" plays out. If you're aggressive, then you'll have to have a Victim to prove how powerful you are.

It actually takes two to play this game. The *Bully* archetype and the *Victim* need each other, otherwise the game cannot be played. Politics plays out in all walks of life, not just within governments but also corporations and even family structure. You can see this playing out in many countries around the world.

Power is addictive and easily corrupts, be it local, national or international. It is insidious within our education system, religion, governments, within families, the prison system, work place bullying, peer groups, different sexual orientations, disabled communities and so on.

Religion fits into this section as well. You automatically believe what the Priest, Rabbi, Minister or Guru is telling you, as you believe that they know more than you do and have powers that you don't.

It never occurs to you to do your own research, or question their knowledge in any way. After all, these structures have been going for thousands of years so it must be true! It's so much easier to accept a doctrine or dogma rather than do your own homework. It takes courage to find out what your own truth is and follow your own inner knowing - we are not taught how to trust ourselves.

Sometimes it's laziness that keeps us from doing this, or the belief that we're too ignorant or simply the sheer presence of the authority figure itself. It can feel very daunting to move away from the tribe and trust your own inner Being to guide you instead. Have you felt this in your life too?

Mainstream, left-brain education sits here as well. Our current education model only serves twenty-five per cent of its students.

As an alternative to the accepted school system, Rudolph Steiner set up a wonderful system in 1919 in Germany, but even that doesn't go far enough these days. Steiner education, (also known via the term Waldorf) emphasizes using our right brain, (where our imagination sits), and integrating this part of our nature with the intellectual and practical side of ourselves. His aim was to provide a holistic education system and currently there are 1050 schools throughout 60 different countries.

One of my children really showed me this in a big way. My younger son was an Indigo child. These children have no idea how to fit into the system; in fact they buck the system whenever they can. When he was three he told me that I couldn't tell him what to do, I wasn't inside his body, I didn't know how he was really feeling! All true of course. I changed schools for him many times thinking the school was the problem; whereas he was the issue because he didn't fit their model. He's totally right brain but I didn't know then what I know now. I'm also sure my parenting model back then was not what it could have been as well, but I wasn't aware of anything else at the time.

These days many terms are used to describe children who do not fit the mainstream model of education. Indigo children first appeared in the 1970's, but now there are other labels such as rainbow, crystal and diamond children. They seem wise beyond their years, may have a fearless approach to life and often very large eyes that seem to look straight through you. But because we don't understand their differences, we label them as A.D.D or A.D.H.D children, or having a condition like Oppositional Defiance Disorder. It's tough being different, as these children do not like conformity; they seem to march to the beat of their own internal drum. They have no respect for anyone who is not in their integrity and just know intuitively who is speaking their truth and who isn't!

WHEN YOU'RE STUCK IN VICTIM MODE

Another unhelpful dynamic is to believe you are often a powerless victim, that someone else is doing something to you, be it your partner, the Government, your parents, your boss, anyone in fact. You need to blame everyone outside of yourself for how your life is looking and you take zero responsibility for anything that unfolds in your reality. The problem with being a *Victim* at the Unconscious level is that if you're ill, then you'll never be able to heal unless you take your power back from external authority figures and beliefs.

Many people are *Victims* and simply not aware that this energy runs them. It's totally normal for them to be blaming others, always finding excuses for their own behavior and usually they feel totally justified in telling others how wrong they are. We all play this role at different times in our lives.

Ruby was adopted and even though her adopted parents did the best job they knew how raising her, she always felt like she was missing out on something. As an adult, she searched for her biological parents, however one had died and the other parent did not want to know of her existence. This just fuelled Ruby's belief that life was unfair, that she had been abandoned and betrayed, even though she knew she was loved and cherished by her adoptive parents. It's easy to understand why Ruby would feel this way, as she did not get any closure around why she was put up for adoption. So her *Victim* feelings did not have any resolution and instead stayed stuck within. Being stuck in the middle of this quandary, it was difficult for her to move on and simply be grateful for the parents she did have.

However, there are other ways to view this scenario, but when you're stuck in *Victim*, it takes a bit of work to move your perceptions about things, so that a different reality can unfold for you. It's not always easy to do, but so worth the effort to move to a higher level of perception. Usually we need help and support to shift this old thinking and find peace within.

POSSESSIONS AND GOALS

Unconsciously, at this level of thinking, you believe that your possessions validate you. You believe you are important because of the car you drive, or the house you live in, even how many degrees you have on the wall. Your whole sense of well being may be dictated by how much money you have in the bank, or who you're in relationship with, perhaps how many children you have. Your Unconscious belief says only when you have it all in place to look like the "Disneyland" map of the world, will your life be fantastic and happy ever after.

Unfortunately, this is a myth and sooner or later a crisis will occur and therefore opportunities arise to prove this perception is false, if you're open to it or ready for it. There's nothing like a stroke, heart attack or cancer to level this playing field. Many wealthy people die alone and miserable, as they believe money is the only important thing in life. The opposite side to this is that you're not safe or allowed to make much money because that will separate you out from your family pattern that believes in "lack!" Money is still a very powerful energy on this planet and used to control and manipulate billions of people.

I find a lot of people agree with the notion of taking responsibility for their actions, as long as it doesn't affect them personally. They often express what others should be doing or how they should be acting! Once it becomes a reality in their own lives however, then their core beliefs come to the surface and the *Victim* arises with the need to blame others for their current situation.

What did you learn about money or possessions? How has this belief driven your life?

Is this scenario familiar to you: the big businessman who thinks they're important because they wield power but then they have to retire? It's not uncommon to hear that they've died a year or two later, or become quite ill, because their belief in their worth or power was totally tied up in their job.

Or how about the talented sportsperson who makes it to the top, but then gets an injury and can no longer compete or play.

Often this situation leads to deep depression and/or drugs. This may be because their whole identity is tied up in their achievements, the accolades and the prestige. They identify with their role and nothing more. This is a very dangerous place to put your self worth.

WHAT WERE YOU TAUGHT ABOUT FEELINGS?

Being Tribal or Unconscious means feelings don't have any importance in your life as it's all about what you think! This is often because you were raised this way to believe only in the scientific world. Perhaps your childhood was so painful at some level, that the only way to survive was to shut down your feelings, put the lid on them, and turn to the rational, functional, left-brain world instead to support you. Is this what you experienced?

While still Unconscious, we're often fed the belief in sacrifice and martyrdom. You serve others even when you're exhausted and having nothing left because that's what the *Good Girl/Boy* does! It never occurs to you to say no, as the fear of not being loved or valued any more creates internal havoc. Invariably you don't listen to the whispers in this scenario (feeling uncomfortable or not at ease), so you have to hear a shout (some sort of illness). The fear of the Unknown is greater than the trauma of the Present.

OLD ADDICTIONS

Our addictions sit here as well and it's not outlandish to say that we all run at least ten addictions. I can hear most people saying, well that's not true of me! Maybe, but we're often not aware of the subtleties of what we're addicted to.

Our addictive behavioral patterns arise out of the feeling that we're not safe, we're not loved enough or the world doesn't look the way I want it to. When these feelings arise within us (often at the unconscious level), then we have to turn to something to make us feel better, even if it's temporary.

In my humble opinion, as adults, our three biggest addictions used to be (and for some people still are) **money, sex, and food**, because they're all major love substitutes.

Money is "God" on this planet at the moment, but I truly believe it will change one day. It wields enormous power because it gives authority to a select few. It's just energy and is every bit as available to you as your next breath, but the fear that comes with lack of money is huge.

Having said that, you can have millions in your bank account, and still live in a miserly way, believing that you'll never have enough or it's not safe to share it around, or it won't be replaced.

Sex is used as a bargaining power for both men and women to get their needs met and is so grossly misconstrued in the commercial world as to be laughable.

Both men and women desire to be touched and held lovingly. You may well have received it as a baby and youngster, but then puberty hits and it all stops! Mixed messages about our sexuality are huge. Sexy images are used to sell cars, caravans, food, clothing or accessories.

In many parts of the world, sex is still used in a brutal way to overpower and intimidate. We still have a long way to go before our sexuality is used in a sacred and loving manner, but until we're taught that we're energetic Beings and shown how to use energy wisely, on all levels, then it will remain misused.

Food, as a love substitute, used to be the domain of women, but men have caught up and the obesity levels on the planet, particularly in the west, are frightening.

When we experience a lack of love in our childhood, we have to turn to something that makes us feel nurtured and cared for. What happened in your childhood when something untoward happened? Were you given something to eat to placate you, or a treat to take your mind off the hurt or pain?

We often learn from an early age that eating something nice or sweet makes us feel better, temporarily at least. It doesn't take long for this to move into an addiction as we crave more and more sweetness in our lives to make up for the emotional and mental pain inside. I know, as I used to be a Chocoholic!

So money, sex and food have been used as love substitutes for eons. So what messages did you receive from your parents or culture about sex, money and food?

NEW ADDICTIONS

Currently, from my experience over the last forty years, I now believe our three major addictions are **social media, busyness, and over thinking.**

In my map of the world, these have become modern day Archetypes that are a sign of the times. They are all a force to be reckoned with.

Social Media

Social media as in Facebook, Twitter, Instagram and all the many other forms are totally seductive and insidious. As with everything in life, there are wonderful things that happen with social media, but it's also used as a control mechanism to compare your life to others. Facebook implies you're important because you have ten thousand friends, yet the reality is the vast majority of it is totally superficial. It feeds the ego as the need to be noticed and approved of takes over.

It can do huge psychological damage to impressionable minds, and like a lot of tabloid media, promotes instant gratification. It's a sign of the times and if you're in the business world, then it's necessary, but it's very tricky to navigate in terms of boundaries and not use it as an avoidance mechanism.

Do you find yourself looking at Social Media and hours have passed and you're still glued to the screen? Some teenagers have a massive addiction to gaming and the future consequences are frightening.

There's a current term called Screenagers, which is self-explanatory really. It's the teenagers who become addicted to their screens. But this addiction is impacting on kids who are five to ten years of age! Children go to bed with their screens, phones or other devices next to them. There is strong research out now that shows the Electric Magnetic Frequencies that come from these devices can strongly alter brain waves and harm young minds.

It's likely that we'll have a group of young adults that will have no idea how to communicate except through their screens. Unless they learn real communication skills at home, this is an art that is likely to be lost.

Busyness

Busyness is a huge addiction for many of us. If you're not busy all the time, doing something important like trying to save the world or perhaps rescuing others then you're not worthwhile somehow or other! Maybe saving the animals, or accruing wealth, or making a difference consumes you? This belief system in busyness has to come from somewhere.

There are numerous, wonderful worthwhile projects on this planet, in fact, a plethora of them. What's important to recognize here is the balance and the motivation behind the busyness.

Are you busy all the time because it fills a void, or perhaps too frightened to confront an important relationship, or is it a form of running away from something? This links into social media very well actually, as they both support each other in terms of busyness.

Maybe your family life keeps you extremely busy with kids and their activities, or you have ageing parents who need help. These passages in our lives are very valid. However it's the choice we make to still keep on being busy when we have an opportunity to slow down that is the issue. We decide to keep being busy, as we don't know how to simply BE with ourselves

I've excelled in Busyness in the past. In fact, the hardest thing ever for me to do on this planet was to STOP and sit still. I almost had to sit on my hands to stop myself from getting up and "doing" things. This is so true for many of us who are or have been Workaholics. The trick is to see behind the belief of why we have to work so hard or keep so busy all the time!

Overthinking Mind

Our last major addiction is to our Mind and always living in our heads. We have been taught that we're only our minds and why not, this is the mind realm after all. However, we're not our mind, it's simply a tool, it's a computer, and it's a program. The truth never has and never will sit in our mind.

It can only contain what has already been fed into it and so much of what has been put into our mind is false. Thoughts such as you're not good enough, you'll never achieve anything worthwhile, or you'll only succeed in the world if you have at minimum of two degrees!

While practical and creative mind are totally necessary, we tend to over think everything and simply think for thinking's sake.

Today with Artificial Intelligence and Augmented Intelligence it's quite overwhelming to think how our lifestyles may be taken over by robots in the future. Predictions say that by 2030, eight hundred million jobs will be redundant.

However, I also believe that our hearts will guide us home. This is another reason why our right brain has to come into equality with our left.

According to Educator Jack Ma, at the World Economic Forum in 2018, we have to change our education platform from knowledge based to "soft skills." In other words, focus on the things a robotic machine can't do! Things like sport, music and art. Jack says we need to teach things like Values, Believing, Teamwork, and Love for others as well as Independent Thinking.

Are we ever taught how to be present, in the moment, with no thought at all? How to simply be present with nature, with a beloved animal, with children? This is a skill we would do well to develop.

The only place that truth sits is in our own heart, but where are we taught to find it there? Perhaps an enlightened parent may guide us to this truth, but I don't know many of them! Some schools now have meditation as part of their curriculum, which is a great place to start awareness training.

Thankfully, with the explosion of quantum physics, plus wonderful studies and organisations like Epigenetics and the HeartMath Institute, the scientific world is gradually catching up to the understanding that we're energetic beings first and foremost.

HeartMath founder Doc Childre's vision, since the 1980's, has been demonstrating to people that harnessing the intelligence of the heart can reduce the cycle of ongoing stress in our lives. But there are still a lot of mainstream scientists that struggle with this belief and look to debunk it. My suggestion would be to try it first, then reject it if it doesn't work for you.

Nevertheless, there are many highly gifted, talented scientists, professors, doctors and scholars who travel around the world educating us to this different reality.

Our Tribal/Unconscious minds are indeed very limited in understanding the true vastness of who we really are. At the Unconscious level, what I've just said is often still seen as questionable, maybe a lie, or even evil in some cultures.

Other Addictions

Maybe you're addicted to sport or to television? How about to education, to retail therapy or to alcohol?Perhaps always being ill or drugs of any sort? Or maybe you're addicted to being in control, or you have to be in charge of everything? How about having a drama filled life all the time?

Perhaps you have a need to be right, or seek attention, or could it be to having power? Maybe it's to being poor (believe it or not)? Could it be telling others what to do, or seeing your psychiatrist weekly? Perhaps you have to keep working all the time because stopping is scary? Maybe it's to keep up a certain identity or social image? The list is endless.

I've noticed quite a lot of older people are actually addicted to suffering, via the *Martyr*. They have lived a life of pain and suffering for so long, they cannot contemplate a life without it. Even if you try to help them in some way, they simply pay lip service to this help and just go back to what is an old habit pattern. Yet they're totally unconscious around this behavior even when it is pointed out to them. They will continuously justify why their life is the way it is.

My mother is the classic example of this. She will not turn the heating on when it's cold, but sit there with numerous rugs around her. She can easily afford to turn the heating on, but it's the *Martyr* pattern within her that just puts up with certain conditions. She often has blue hands in the winter, literally because of the cold house she lives in. But she refuses to hear that it's because of the cold that her hands are blue, sometimes even black! It's been proven to her on numerous occasions than when in a warm environment her hands do not discolor. But she just goes back to her rigid way of thinking and will not allow any other possibility to enter her way of thinking.

Others of us are addicted to feelings like guilt or shame. This will be hard to believe for some people, but therapists all over the world will validate this statement. Then of course there's the strong universal belief that I'm not enough in some way or other. It's often embedded into our childhood experiences and I come across many adults in their forties, fifties and sixties who still adhere to this belief. It's a huge list and requires honesty to sort it out, but at the Tribal/Unconscious level, that's not likely to happen.

CHILD ARCHETYPE – TRIBAL/UNCONSCIOUS LEVEL

The Unconscious *Child* needs to blame everyone for what's happening in their life if it's not what they want. They may feel life is too hard and someone else should make it easier for them. Many times they're lazy or they may have no idea how to express themselves. They have trouble asking clearly for their needs to be met, which usually means their life will play out in a series of dramas.

They usually see the glass as half empty, (never half full) and will easily get angry when things don't go their way. The Child will either become timid or the flip side to this is to become the bully. They are often emotionally unavailable or switched off completely from their feelings.

They are usually not present in their body, often in their head or away with the "pixies." *"The lights are on, but no-one is at home!"* When things get tough they may hold onto a rigid perspective, as they struggle to be flexible.

Metaphorically speaking, the Child wants to hide in the corner until the problem has gone away. The Child will usually have a huge problem with saying "I'm sorry" or admitting any "wrong" doing. The Child just wants to be happy and make it a reality immediately; however, they usually don't wish to put any work into making this happen.

The main component that underlies nearly everything at the Unconscious level is **fear.** It calls the shots with practically everything that happens. There's simply no awareness that this is the case.

So what happens to move you out of this way of believing this reality is the truth? Keep reading.

5

THE GIFT OF THE CRISIS –
INDIVIDUATION

Moving from the Unconscious way of living, where we operate out of automaticity, usually takes a crisis. We all experience crises in our lives, but some of us do so with more drama than others. There are crises so huge that we never recover from them, like floods, fires, earthquakes, cancer, heart attacks, strokes, let alone the death of a parent or child.

The crisis may be the break up of a marriage, loss of a job and income, or moving half way around the world for example. It can push us into the "dark night of the soul" and for some of us we stay there forever. We may become frozen in our terror and grief.

This Sub-conscious or Individuation level is typified by two words: CHAOS and MADNESS. It can feel like this when you're thrust into this area, as it's not something you'd ever choose for yourself consciously! You may feel very alone, deserted or betrayed by something or someone.

Kevin was a young man of nineteen who loved life and lived it to the full. However, one night Kevin got on his motorbike to go and get something from the corner store. He did not come back in the same condition he left. He crashed and became a quadriplegic! His whole world collapsed.

It took years for him to learn how to function again. This man has employed the *Pioneer* to the hilt. Now in his forties, he has flown solo in a modified plane all over the country, paddled a modified kayak for three thousand kilometres, been in the Para Olympics, got married, worked full time and is loved by anyone who comes to know him. His attitude and approach to life is inspirational.

Kevin proves that it's possible to overcome the chaos and madness when the crisis hits. It took conscious effort on his part to make this decision to live his life this way. It didn't happen immediately of course, he had to go through the grief of no longer having his young, vibrant body anymore, but through the gift of this crisis, he has become a source of magnificent motivation to many others who are going through their own crises.

Let's look back a bit - it may be that you remember vividly your first day of primary school and felt very alone, frightened and unsure of yourself. You may have experienced something similar on your first day of secondary school. These are little crises that we have to overcome and we usually do. But others are huge and not so easily dealt with, like the death of a child, sibling or parent, the appalling school massacres that happen in some countries or walking away from a toxic family.

We had a shocking fire in Melbourne in 2009, which was labeled Black Saturday. More than four hundred bushfires started on this day, with the highest ever loss of life where one hundred and seventy three people died and more than one hundred people were taken to hospital with severe burns.

Years later I met Pete who had lost everything that day - his property, his livestock, his wife, and his whole life as he'd known it wiped out in one day. Like so many others who suffered through that day his loss was unbearable and inconceivable. Pete was the true definition of the *Hero* on this day as he tried to save everything he could. In fact, so many people played out the *Hero/Heroine* on this day as often happen when human nature is put to the test.

But the thing that was remarkable about Pete was his acceptance of this shocking tragedy. He'd always lived on the land, knew the vagaries of Mother Nature well and over time, accepted that it was all beyond his control. He could either move into massive resentment of what happened or learn to accept it, grieve and move on with his life. He did not shut down his heart, instead he was instrumental in helping others re-establish their own properties, as well as his own. He lived in the belief that some things are not easily understood and are difficult to comprehend, but he chose to move on in his life with trust and love in his heart.

So what crises in life have you experienced, both big and little? Remember, what's big to you may seem little to someone else, as it's all perception, but it's still real and often terrifying. I've had many in my life, but somehow, these all seem minor compared to what others go through. Every single crisis is an opportunity for growth.

PERHAPS IT'S A GIFT

The gift of the crisis is how we deal with it and our attitude towards it. Of course, you may not be able to look at it this way when you're in the middle of it, but perhaps at some point down the track, you may be open to another perspective. It can mean the start of your journey into self-development and awareness, or living your life very differently to how you've done in the past.

The gift of the crisis may mean that finally you've had enough pain and you want to live your life more harmoniously. It may be time to change your life financially, or in relationships, perhaps emotionally, or to adopt a different set of values and ethics.

This is the time to turn fear based Archetypes around and use them positively in your life. But it's a choice. Can you choose to take off the old glasses that only saw life through the lens of doom and gloom and put on new glasses that say, "Anything is possible if I can change my attitude?"

Maybe you've been working for someone who doesn't mind ripping people off, and finally you can't live with that anymore, as your own personal integrity is worth more to you than being in a job that justifies this. Perhaps you're living a lie in your marriage and you stay there to keep others safe or keep up a public image of being the perfect couple!

Sooner or later, our intuition or gut knowing will push us to the edge of conscience or consciousness and ask us to do it differently. For some of us, the fear of change will cripple us mentally, emotionally or physically, so change will not happen. For others, they will take a leap of faith and trust themselves enough to live a different life.

There's no rule here as to when to make change. It will happen when it's ready to happen and not a second before. Many of us go back over and over for the same lesson until we've finally had enough and are wise enough to finally make a move. This is true for many of us when we're dealing with relationship issues.

STAYING SAFE

As I mentioned earlier, we simply don't move, grow or change when we're in a comfort zone. We love our comfort zones! We strive for them and just want to stay in them. But ask yourself this question:

When did the most growth, change and expansion come into your life - when you were in a comfort zone or when you were forced to make changes?

For most of us, it will be the latter.

Too many of us struggle in allowing change to be made willingly or consciously, as it's one of our biggest fears. So the majority of us unconsciously invite the crisis into our lives to give us an opportunity to look at life differently. But the fear that arises can be all consuming.

Bill was in a difficult job. He hated getting up in the morning and going to work, but he stayed there because he needed to support his family. Common story really. Eventually he became quite ill, with a muscular condition, which meant it was very hard for him to walk, let alone go to work. The medical model wanted to put him on a plethora of drugs, but he researched the side effects of these drugs and decided that pathway wasn't for him.

So we did a chart reading over the phone. Among other archetypes, what came up were the *Judge, Leader* and *Worrier*. It was very clear that he was not listening to his inner guidance and instead was ruled by his fears and beliefs that said he must keep on going, even if he hated his job and it was killing him (*Worrier* Archetype). It was time to lead in another direction (*Leader*) and instead of judging this situation through fear based eyes, use his inner discernment and wisdom to discover a deeper truth from within (*Judge*).

This is exactly what Bill's father had done too: stayed at a job that wore him down until he was a shell of his former self. Now Bill was in the same boat. He had a major choice to make: be true to himself or continue in the same direction that his father had taken. He was totally at the crossroads in his life and it was his health that forced the issue. So many of us do it this way as it's only when our health becomes an issue that we pay attention! Most of us get to a point where we have to make inner choices if we want to live a fulfilling life.

THE FEAR OF BEING OUT OF CONTROL

In my map of the world, our number one fear is our fear of **being out of control.** Just play with this scenario for a few moments - in the womb, you knew who you were. You knew you were connected at all times to Source or Infinite Potential. You had all your needs supplied. The only downside was that it got a bit crowded towards the end.

Then you're born into a human body and either at birth, or just after birth you experience something called Vital Shock. That's when it occurs to you that you're this helpless little soul, totally reliant on everyone for your well being. At that point, you will experience a sense of fear that you're not safe and your needs may not be met. Does this scenario make sense?

This can play out all of your life, in different ways and at varying times. However we all experience this to a minor or major degree, as we all take on board a body.

Some babies are born into a crisis of life situation – perhaps the chord is wrapped around their neck or the placenta has dislodged, or perhaps the mother is very ill. Sometimes these babies are put into Intensive Care, taken away from their mothers and have to struggle to live and thrive. These traumas set up shock in the baby's body and may continue to play out in some way or another for the rest of this person's life. It resurrects itself every time a situation occurs that seems life threatening in some way.

The body remembers at a cellular level that it's not safe, so will respond in Fight/Flight mode and can lead to many different health situations like adrenal exhaustion or a poor immune system,

Thankfully there are things you can do to offset this like Osteopathy, Hypnosis, Kinesiology, Trauma Release and so on - this is discussed later in the book.

YOUR FIRST FEAR BASED MEMORY

So at some point, your fear of being **out of control** kicks in, at the Unconscious level. Perhaps it was the first time you lost your parent in a supermarket, or the first time you couldn't find your teddy bear, or maybe the first time you were left with a stranger? It's all perception after all. You will experience fear and therefore the feeling that you're not safe.

Some children have a totally brutal parent or parents and this fear of being out of control will run them for the rest of their lives. Hopefully, at some point, they wake up that this is not a kind loving way to live, so decide to take their power back from this fear based belief system and choose not to play this game anymore.

It's nearly impossible to do this as children of course, as you do not possess the discernment skills or maturity levels necessary to make a change, so generally it takes becoming an adult and life getting so hard that only at rock bottom will these different choices be made. It's sad that it has to be this way, but it's usually the way it goes.

DEEPER PURPOSE

The deeper purpose of a crisis is to ask some very important questions of the Inner You.

> *What is going on in your life that you've attracted or invited in this level of chaos, madness, mayhem or drama?*

> *What is your Higher Consciousness or intuition trying to tell you?*

> *Where is your thinking at? How are you really feeling on the inside?*

> *What are you **not** owning or **not** saying?*

> *What do you **not** want to look at or address?*

These are deep questions that will lead to self-empowerment or self-awareness.

If you cast a chart around these questions, then you will get your answers, or it may be that your heart speaks its truth clearly to you and therefore a chart may be affirming of what your heart is already saying to you.

Unfortunately, you won't be able to ask these questions if you have a strong *Victim* at the Unconscious level because you'll need to blame everyone else for what's happening in your life. It may well take till the crisis has passed before you can ask yourself these questions, as they can simply be too hard to ask when you're in the middle of something huge. It takes courage to ask these inward focused questions and not everyone has this level of courage. You must have, or you wouldn't be reading this book!

A crisis may mean that you're at the cross roads in your life. It may mean that your Higher Self – the wise part of you that we all have, that is all loving, all knowing, all compassionate – is trying to get your attention to say, "*Look again*, this way is not working for you!"

RUNNING OLD THOUGHTS

When we're in this Sub-Conscious area, we tend to run old thoughts that no longer serve us. Being at the cross roads is the wise part of you waving a huge red flag saying **pay attention**, you're sticking to an old pathway but it doesn't serve you anymore.

The wise part of you that I'll call the *Sage/Crone* Archetype within is saying, take the new pathway, but this of course requires inner conviction and courage. The *Sage/Crone* aspect of you comes from your heart, gives you wonderful guidance and direction, but you have to learn how to listen to it. It talks to you via your intuition, your gut knowing, and your inner radar.

We all have this, but the scientific world can negate it. You have many different Archetypes that also give you this helpful information, but where are you taught to find them?

The thinking part of you will be saying, "Yes, I want to walk a new pathway but first give me the gilt edged guarantee that I can't make a fool of myself and nothing will go wrong. I want it to be one hundred per cent successful, knowing everything will turn out just fine!"

This is you bargaining internally between your mind and your heart. Your Higher Self (that part of you that has all knowledge, all wisdom, all love, all compassion) doesn't work that way. It wants you to take the leap of faith first and the proof usually drops in afterwards.

So which part of yourself will you listen to? The mind part of you, that is only based on old thinking (it can't do anything else) or the heart part of you that wants another pathway as it knows the old pathway no longer serves you.

There is no way I was capable of taking this new pathway until I started on the self-development/spiritual component of my life, in my thirties. Before that I was way too Unconscious (this is not a judgment, it's simply a fact). I was too caught up in marriage, children, socializing and work, to the extent that I was totally unaware that a bigger picture even existed. I'm very grateful for the many crises I've experienced in my life, both big and small as they have all taught me a lot.

It is extremely heartening to me to see the amount of aware children that are around these days, because their parents (now in their thirties and forties) have much more wisdom and consciousness than I ever had at a similar age.

Sometimes I've gone back over and over again for the same lesson, but hey, some of us are slow learners! I've just kept on recycling the old thinking. Maybe you do the same? These days I catch a glimpse of something being off center and I can usually correct it before the crisis needs to unfold. That's the benefit of growth work and endeavoring to become Conscious.

Now I get strong bodily messages or dreams if something does not serve me. I've learned how to listen to my intuition and follow the whispers, so the shouts are usually no longer necessary.

A POWERFUL TRUE STORY

I know a wonderful man called John Coleman. He was diagnosed with advanced Parkinson's Disease and early stage Multi-system Atrophy and told that his future held more debilitating symptoms, increasing dependence on pharmaceutical medication and, eventually, full-time care. He decided he didn't want to follow the doctor's predictions for his remaining life, so he set out to find his own way. He is one of the increasing numbers of people to recover from this illness and do it his way. He wrote a couple of terrific books, the first one is called *Stop Parkin' and Start Livin' - reversing the symptoms of Parkinson's disease,* and the second one is *Shaky Past* (his autobiography). He's currently writing a third book.

It took John facing his own mortality to make a huge decision – he started to see all the things he'd avoided dealing with and set about putting his life in balance, using a combination of alternative healing modalities, as well as forgiveness and gratitude. This is how some people embrace the crisis, but not all of us can do this.

WILL YOU ACCEPT THIS GIFT?

The Crisis itself is an opportunity to do things differently, if you're open and willing to make change. It's asking you to stop being busy, pay attention to your inner being and check out what's going on inside. You'll never get to this level of clarity if you're constantly darting from one place to another, with never a spare second in your day. Busyness is the ultimate distraction to personal growth and exploration, yet we all do it, as it's so acceptable.

The Subconscious area can be a scary place because one part of you knows that something is not right, but the other part wants you to stay doing "same old, same old." This is the battle between your mind and your heart. Your mind will say to you, "Stay safe, don't rock the boat." But your heart will say, "You're ready, take a leap of faith!" Which part of yourself you listen to can depend on where your inner *Child* is sitting in your chart.

The Child's biggest fear is change and being out of control, so even if your current circumstances are unpalatable, the Child doesn't care because it would rather have the familiar and known compared to the unknown. Does this sound familiar? This is the case if your inner Child is at the Unconscious level.

When this difficult scenario is going on in our lives, often our first thought is to run back to the Tribe, Culture or Group, turn to one of our many addictions such as busyness, alcohol, food, drugs, movies, books and so on to make us feel better and numb out. We all do this at some point in our lives.

Or perhaps we'll be so busy blaming everyone for where we're at, that anger, bitterness and revenge consume us and we can't see any future but this old way of thinking.

This dilemma or level of awareness often means the start of the journey from our mind to our heart. At this level it can be exhausting because the dilemma is internal, not external. It's a necessary part of our growth and there's no escaping this level, it's akin to serving our apprenticeship – no one can do it for you, you must go through this to get to the other side.

Think of every inspiring story you've ever read or heard about, there is always a struggle to move from an old way of being to a new, unknown way of living life. This is the journey of human existence. You have the courage within, but you may have to dig deep to find it.

CHILD ARCHETYPE – SUB CONSCIOUS OR INDIVIDUATION LEVEL

If your Child is sitting here, then you will be plagued with doubts, such as: will I/ won't I or should I/shouldn't I?? The inner battle is going on between your mind and your heart and it can truly drive you nutty if this goes on for a long time.

It's almost like a battle of wills between the wise part of yourself that wants you to move forward and the frightened *Child* part that wants everything to stay the same, because it's familiar. We all get to this part in our lives at some point, around many different issues. The choices we make depend upon our level of tolerance around our pain and suffering.

The answer is to understand that a lot of our inherited beliefs are fear based. The answer is to examine them and pull them apart. Don't take my word for this, or anyone else's either! Do your own homework so that you become empowered to live your authentic life, living in your integrity and openness, so that the inner and outer aspects of yourself match.

If you do this, you can then drop doubting mind and wake up to the understanding of your own true nature. Why wouldn't you do this? Why wouldn't you find out who you really are compared to the old programs you've received and taken on board?

The motivation behind this Subconscious realm is to help you to fully wake up and become Conscious, move you onto the next level of Awareness, because this is where your real joy sits. Not fleeting, momentary joy, but permanent aliveness that permeates every cell of your Being. Do you want this?

6

LIVING YOUR JOY - SYMBOLIC

I totally believe this capacity to live our joy is within every single one of us and that we're all connected to the one Source energy, no matter what you like to call it. There are many gifted Beings on the planet today, who help us to realize our own true nature is LOVE and not the greed and misuse of power that is so prevalent for all to see.

When we're looking at this level of Consciousness, we're talking about the state of the Realised Being, like Christ, Buddha, Lao Tsu, Muhammad, Sri Ramana Maharshi, Osho, Papaji, Adi Da, or Sri Mooji, (to name a few) all those evolved Souls that have come to this planet, at different times, to help us understand who we really are. There is a plethora of literature available to read about these Beings, their lives and their wisdom.

These fully Conscious, Enlightened Beings seem worlds away compared to us ordinary mortals. But that too is a belief system. We've thought that way for thousands of years but it's not the truth. It's time to really find out who you are.

TAKING FULL RESPONSIBILITY

At this Conscious level of Awareness, you take full responsibility for what's going on in your life. There is no need to blame anyone else as you remember, at the cellular level, that you wrote this script before you decided to incarnate into this body.

Sometimes, when I'm with a client, I'm shown their other lifetimes and given information on the reasons behind why they wrote this particular script for themselves. It always seems to tie in with the Archetype Chart and make sense.

Because of this, I've come to understand that all the people in your life have acted out the roles you gave them before incarnation, (painful, benign or loving), as they were providing you with a platform of experiences from which you were meant to move on.

The Halliday family explains this concept really well. Mum and Dad were *High Achievers,* so they worked all the time. The children saw their parents at weekends basically and did not get the emotional support or quality time they needed with their parents while growing up. We tend to either follow in the footsteps of our parents, or go in the opposite direction. In this case, the kids emulated their parents and became *High Achievers* too.

However, the kids were both internally unhappy (although the outside looked fine to the public) so the son turned to drugs to placate his unhappiness and the daughter turned to food. Eventually, after looking to food to give her the comfort and love she was really craving, the bottom line in dissatisfaction was reached. This meant that the daughter started to wake up about the role models she received around being the *High Achiever.* She questioned the values she was living by. She began to see why she was eating so much and realized she used food to stuff down her emotions and keep them at arm's length.

She finally felt the pain around her childhood, got in touch with her deepest desires and passions, and started to pursue them. The chart showed her how many times she had put off living her life and fulfilling her dreams.

So her parents gave her the role model of what NOT to do and it was her task to say thanks, but no thanks and go and live her life the way her heart wanted her to. The same applies to the son of course.

There's great freedom in understanding this. It takes you out of the drama, brings in your Higher Self (that wise part of you) and opens you up to new possibilities that are yet to unfold. This can be very exhilarating as you stop trying to control everything with your mind and let the heart take the front seat.

I've experienced many examples of this. Whenever I've had an issue with someone, I no longer try to work it out. I just link my Higher Self with that person's Higher Self and ask the Universe to give me the perfect opportunity (and wisdom to do so) to speak my truth, so that **both** of us will be heard and understood.

Without fail, this always works. I may have to wait only a day, or it could be a year but the perfect timing is always given to me.

I remember the time my father was dying of cancer. I was shown in meditation that I needed to help him cross over, so that he could die in peace. My father was an atheist. The problem was that my mother and father were cloned at the hip. They did everything together. My mother used to cut short any talk of death or dying as well as anything that could mean feelings may arise.

So I handed it over at the High Self level and waited. I used to stay with them when I was visiting from the country. I would be cleaning my teeth in the bathroom and I'd hear the words: "Go in and talk to your father NOW." I would sometimes have only ten minutes before I'd hear my mother's footsteps. She was coming to see what we were talking about and decide if she agreed with it.

In that ten minutes it was amazing what words I was given, how the conversation unfolded so quickly and deeply and how his fears could be offset by a deeper truth.

I need to mention at this point that my parents had no idea what my work was or what I've done over the last forty years. They never wanted to know, so I didn't tell them, so this conversation with my father was a complete surprise to him. These "sneaky" conversations happened a number of times, but the Higher Self was in charge of it all. I was very grateful and blessed to be given this opportunity to serve my father in this way.

Perhaps this is all too much for you to take on board right now? If this is so, that's fine, just throw these examples in one of your baskets.

INTUITION

We all have intuition, (not necessarily psychic gifts), but the critical issue is do we use our intuition and if so, do we trust it?

This Intuitive skill has helped me a lot to understand the significance of the various roles people have played in my lifetime.

When my beautiful daughter was young, she unknowingly treated me like a servant. I was shown our lifetimes together and the higher purpose of us being together. Seeing and experiencing this information helped me take our relationship to another level. We are each other's teachers and I feel incredibly blessed to have her in my life. She operates so easily at a heart level, teaching Aware Parenting, and as a Doula has helped new parents give birth in a loving and conscious manner. She has totally learned how to accept responsibility for herself, her actions and her beliefs and to me, is a very wise being.

Our intuitive gifts really start to open up at this Conscious or Symbolic level, as it's our heart and right brain that are predominant in this column. But sometimes we're not ready or we don't know how to use these gifts wisely when they start to open up.

This was my experience in my mid thirties and it scared me. Thankfully, my ex husband supported me and said go and explore this new phenomena. I will always be grateful to him for his encouragement back then.

I've come across many people over the last forty years or so who have different abilities, but learn how to hide them, excuse them or belittle them as their family of origin find them weird, evil or too confronting. Maybe this happened to you too? When these people find someone on their wavelength, it's a huge joy for them.

At this Conscious place of understanding, fear no longer calls the shots, so you own your natural and intuitive gifts (which we all have), which means you stop apologising for them and instead use them for the highest good of all.

DISCERNMENT

It is a wise soul who knows whom to confide in, share with and experience different realities. It is important to have non-judgmental people around you who are open to hearing and listening to you.

I've had many wake up calls around this lesson called discernment. In the past, I've broken bones when I've done something because the *Good Girl* within did the right thing, went out to a dinner just to please others, slipped, fell and injured myself. These days, I have way more discernment and cancel things if they do not feel right.

KNOWING YOUR ALLIES

The Archetypes become your Ally if you're living in this field of awareness. They are your friend and give you the whispers very clearly regarding changing direction, or perhaps suggest you need to look at your integrity issues. They support you in finding the courage to make the necessary changes in your life.

So far I've been explaining how the Archetypes can trip you up if you're not paying attention. Now it's time to understand that they can serve you enormously when you learn to work with them. Perhaps you do a chart for yourself and the *Weaver* comes up, along with the *Artist,* both at the Symbolic or Conscious level.

This is how your Higher Self is telling you that you have all the skills necessary to weave together the changes that are necessary for your highest good. The wise part of you is saying that it's now time to write your new script or paint your new picture, coming from the wisdom of your heart, fearlessly, going within and trusting yourself.

The Archetypes may come to you via your dreams or your intuition. They may be experienced as flashes of insight, even in surprising places like the supermarket or cleaning the toilet. I know many people who get their "flashes" while they're under the shower. Somehow or other water acts as a conduit for their intuition. Perhaps it's simply gut knowing or a clear heart bodily response to a suggestion.

I know one lady, Claire, who every time she wants higher guidance about an issue, goes and does a ceremony for herself. She lights incense, burns candles, gives an offering of fruit to the Earth Mother and then sits and meditates. It works for her every time.

Often when I'm given insights as to what to do next, my whole body responds by tingling all over, from top to toe. I cannot make this happen, it's a natural phenomenon. Instead of calling it goose bumps, some people call this body tingling, truth bumps! Has this happened to you?

Isobel had to find the courage to bring about changes in her life. She knew she needed to be true to herself. She left a dysfunctional relationship and moved into a new house with her daughter. She left a job that was slowly but surely destroying her, and found a Spiritual teacher whom she resonated with. Isobel had always been aware she felt empty on the inside and realized finally that the only person who could fill this emptiness was herself.

Isobel was taught how to drop into her heart, let go of her mind and busyness and find the truth within. Her life started to flow with synchronicities happening everywhere and at last her well being and joy were coming from inside. She even told all her friends that she would no longer be socializing with them, or having the regular coffee morning. Isobel found she could no longer do mindless chatter about situations that held no interest for her, or gossip about others.

She felt very happy about this turn of events and of course, still saw those people with whom she had a heart connection but Isobel could no longer show up because it was the "right" thing to do, or run the fear of what others would think of her if she didn't.

She stopped caring what the outside world thought of her. Instead her inner child became conscious and Isobel simply lived her life by being true to herself. She still had hard, physical work to do, looking after her own property, but there was an internal, underlying joy now to everything that unfolded in her life.

BEYOND YOUR FIVE SENSES

At this stage of your life, you understand that you're so much more than what you've been taught. That this earth plane is not the only form of "intelligent" life. Are we really intelligent with all that we've done to ourselves via wars, greed, power and destruction?

You become aware that you're much more than your five senses, in fact, you get that you're a multi dimensional Being. You understand at this level what it's like to be in your heart centre, to be in the zone and to experience higher guidance or Consciousness as you chose to live from this place.

You attract in your "soul" family at this level, which may not be your biological family. By this I mean people who are on the same wavelength as you, people you can easily relate to and who accept you exactly the way you are. You share similar experiences, understandings and philosophies. You're also very open to what others have to say: you no longer need to judge anyone and their pathway in life. Love and acceptance is the name of the game while being authentic and in your integrity.

You may find you resonate differently with those who are still at the Unconscious level. However, you're not coming from a place of judgment, but from a place of acceptance that all is the way it's meant to be. You realize that others will "wake up" when it's their time to do so. You understand that we're all from the one Unified Source anyway, so there's no need to control anything at all as others have their own unique pathway to walk.

Living in this level of Consciousness does not condone violence or aggression in any form, but understands that's not who we truly are. The violence on this planet is a result of what we've been taught and programmed to believe. We need to educate ourselves and wake up to what we're doing. Not just to ourselves, but also to this magnificent planet we live on. Perhaps change our values, learn how to love ourselves and respect others for their differences.

There are many gifted, talented Beings on this planet who live at this level of Consciousness and can bring about great change in people's lives. Eckhart Tolle is one, as is Sri Mooji and Gangaji.

Many tribal Shamans have learned how to access higher levels of Consciousness and therefore affect all sorts of things like weather or illness, change their form (which is called shape shifting) or converse with Nature Spirits, to name just a few possibilities.

However, just because people have these skills, does not mean they are an Awakened Being. You must always use discernment and trust your heart around what feels right for you to do and experience.

This pathway is not for everyone and if this does not resonate with you, then throw this statement into your Rubbish bin.

TRUST AND BEING PRESENT

Unfortunately, we can't go to a Doctor to get trust pills! It's intangible and only comes with maturity and living life. But it's a very necessary quality to have. What do I mean by trust or being present?

When Spirit showed me to build a meditation retreat at Jamieson (Victoria), my first thought was *where's Jamieson?* My second thought was, *with what?* as we'd just been wiped out financially (with my first husband).

I learned many lessons from building this meditation retreat, such as faith and discernment. Then there was discipline and commitment. These are all necessary attributes that go into Trust.

One of the biggest obstacles I had to overcome was my addiction to busyness. I had to learn how to drop into stillness in spite of the fact that there was so much physical hard work to do. Being still was a vital component to learn. It was through the stillness and meditation I was given all the instructions regarding how to set up the energies on the place to benefit all that visited.

Learning about faith came to me via the old movie of Kevin Costner's, *Field of Dreams*. This movie kept me going and gave me faith when it seemed way too hard to fulfil the dream and make it into a reality. Faith is the deeper knowing within that your pathway is your passion.

To complete a vision or desire, discipline is usually necessary. This is the quality that can bring people undone. It goes like this: "What do you mean I have to get up early to meditate? What do you mean I have to exercise more? What do you mean I have to watch my thoughts and words?"

I could go on and on. It's the discipline factor that is hard for so many, especially the Millennials. They were brought up in an era of instant gratification, so learning discipline may be a hard taskmaster for some of them.

Following the dream through to completion is a real skill. For many, when the going gets tough, they give up. My experience shows me that when I'm given an intuitive hit about something to do, somewhere to go, or something to create, I know that I will usually be tested on my commitment to follow through as obstacles arise.

So I say "yes" immediately if it feels right, then let it unfold. I now see the obstacles for what they are - just the ego/mind having a game with me. When I drop out of the mind's busy-ness and center again in my heart, then ease and grace is given which allows the commitment to come to fruition.

Discernment may mean being wise about whom you share your dream with. Find those people who support you, believe in you, listen to you and also offer wisdom when it's asked for.

SELF LOVE

The thing that epitomizes this level of Consciousness to me is something called **Self Love**. It's a strange concept to many of us, as nowhere are we taught this. At the Unconscious level, we're told it's better to give than receive, and to always put others first. Mothers in particular excel at this. If you do anything other than this, it's considered selfish, particularly by the Tribe. Have you come across this way of thinking?

A classic example of this is if you're running *Martyr* or *Caretaker* at the Unconscious level, then self love will not get a look in as you're too busy taking care of others or living vicariously through different people, usually family. I did not understand this concept until I was in my fifties. I was too busy being busy, achieving, controlling, planning, kids, family, work, entertaining and so on.

Now in my sixties, I crave the still time, the alone time, the ability to drop into the emptiness within and experience a different reality which is more akin to my true nature than what happens in the external world.

I can still do all the other things, but self love is a priority now and I give myself what I need, be it time away on my own, or fun and laughter with friends, stillness and many other things that will fit into this basket.

What you need to do for yourself that equals self love will be unique to you and looks like different things to each age group.

At the Conscious level of Awareness, you understand that unless *Self Love* is at the top of your priority list then everything else is out of balance. I'm not talking about narcissism, I'm talking about valuing yourself as equally important as your partner, your children, the planet, your friends, your family, your work, in fact anything that demands your time.

If you fill your own cup first, to overflowing, then it's easy to give to others, in equality. But if your own cup has nothing in it, then you'll be running on empty and one of the ways to get your attention around this pattern is to become ill.

It's really hard taking these first steps into *Self Love*. It's so strange and foreign for so many of us to put ourselves first that we may become consumed by guilt.

Sharon is one lady who specialized in being a *Servant* to others. This is the role model her mother gave her and her religion strengthened as well. Her wake up call came through illness, as it often does. It became clear that she had no idea about self love or nurturing and what it even meant.

Taking baby steps at first, she gradually started doing enjoyable things for herself, be it time out to meditate, go for walks, body treatments and even going away on her own. It can also mean dropping the judgmental mind, finding compassion for the self, having clear boundaries and being able to say NO without any guilt attached.

Her partner was shocked when Sharon first suggested time out for herself, as she'd never left her husband on his own before. It took courage on Sharon's part to suggest this and then follow it through. Now it's a necessary component in her life as she loves writing and drawing and this gives her the space to be totally creative, write to her heart's content and explore her inner world and express it. Her marriage has grown up and both she and her partner explore their creativity in their own way.

Of course, in my own case, my two biggest addictions have been busyness and surrogating for other people's illnesses. This is the exact opposite to what *Self Love* looks like. But I didn't know any better back then. It's the journey of a lifetime to learn about *Self Love*. In fact, I think it's one of the hardest journeys of all.

Julia was a schoolteacher who taught Art. She was becoming ill on a regular basis. The chart came up with *Villain Crook* and *Trickster*, both strong Archetypes. Julia was over teaching the kids, doing all the administration work and felt stifled in her self expression and what she really wanted to convey on a canvas. But job security and fear of the unknown kept her trapped in her work role.

These Archetypes were asking her to look at how she was ripping herself off and playing games. She had the courage to follow her dream, open up her own art school and has been helping people to fulfil their own artistic dreams ever since. She loves her life, is living her passion and wakes up each day experiencing joy rather than drudgery.

My definition of *Self Love* means using both left and right brains; exploring your creativity; having a great mix between family, work, friends; being still or meditating; knowing when to stop and when to play; being child like with spontaneity and innocence; opening up to the many parts of yourself; and reveling in new experiences.

It means honoring and valuing yourself with self respect, self worth, having good self esteem (I'm not talking about arrogance here which sits at the Unconscious level), living in your integrity, walking your walk, talking your talk, being true to your own pathway and never judging it against someone else's ideal. Listening to your own heart for guidance and then employing your mind with how it needs to unfold. It's summarised by the feeling that we're all spiritual beings having a human experience and not the other way around.

What does *Self Love* look like for you? Are you even aware of it? Do you have any role models for it in your life?

LOVE'S PRESENCE

What about role models for love itself? Hopefully we get to experience a beautiful level of love from our parents, but sadly, not all of us do. Maybe you've been blessed to feel totally loved by a partner or a close friend. It's not a surprise that so many of us turn to the animal kingdom to experience love.

I have a friend called Elisabeth who experiences so much peace and love when she is in her garden. It brings her great joy and she feels it in every cell of her being. Can you relate to this?

For me, heaven on a stick is walking on the beach on a balmy day and feeling the connection with Nature that way. I've often felt on overwhelm as love pours through me when I look at my grandchildren or family members, my partner, friends or animals. It takes my breath away at times.

I love music, especially harmonies and sacred chanting. One of the musical groups I've come across in the last fifteen years is Deva Premal and her partner Miten. They met in the mid 1990's at their spiritual master's Ashram in India. I have been to quite a number of their concerts and sacred chanting retreats. For me, when I'm around these two magnificent Beings, they epitomise to me what Love looks like, of themselves, of each other and all of their audience. The love is palpably felt in their Presence. Their music opens up the heart, allows love to flow and you feel the magnificence of All That Is flowing through you.

In other words, for me, I am in touch with the truth of my Being. Other people experience this feeling when they listen to classical music or go to Symphony Concert.

So how do you experience love? Is it only from others? Can you give it to yourself? Can you feel it when you're in Nature, with your family, friends, playing music, writing, being still, painting, drawing, creating in any way, helping others, or through the animal kingdom? There are no limits on love; it comes in many forms and in different ways. But it is our true nature if we allow it in.

I have done over twenty thousand charts at the time of printing this book. I have never, ever come across anyone who has had all twelve of his or her Archetypes at this Conscious level. This is not to say that they don't exist, I'm just saying I've never done an Archetype Chart Reading for them as I imagine they don't want one or need one at this level.

We catch glimpses of being at this level, but find it hard to maintain all the time because of the mental games that are played. I have no doubt we're all capable of living this way, but only when we understand that the heart is our true nature and not our thinking Mind. We need both of course, but the Heart is the true master.

THE MYSTIC

I've been saying to clients for years, I wish I had two big Mack trucks parked outside my place. One would be filled with *Self Love* pills and the other would be filled with *Trust* pills. The underlying component to live at this level of Awareness is Trust. But where are we taught Trust and how can we live it anyway when the majority of this planet is based on fear?

Trust is earned, learned and absorbed at the deepest level. It comes about when you learn how to listen within, to your heart's highest truth, living as that truth, in integrity and following your intuition. It's actually the Archetype of the *Mystic*, where you learn to live in the world, but not be of this world. It's epitomized by Dumbledore from the Harry Potter movies.

Ironically, Enlightened Beings don't need trust at all, as they live as Love with Spirit flowing through them, totally open and present to whatever needs to unfold.

Being a current day *Mystic* is tough. In the old days, you would be secluded in a monastery and all your needs would be supplied. These days, for most of us, you have to go to work, often look after a family, help others in the community less fortunate than yourself, shop, cook, clean, as well as take care of your own spiritual needs. It's a tall order at times and brings up your commitment to your own growth, self love and the desire to be in Union with Spirit.

Unless you live with the Shamans or true indigenous cultures, or seek out an enlightened Spiritual teacher, it's hard to find someone who can teach you how to do this; it's trial and error all the way along this path and with it comes maturity, wisdom, inner knowing and love of self and others, seeing past the ego and its play, and understanding that there are many unseen levels operating on this earth plane.

THE CONSCIOUS CHILD ARCHETYPE

The *Child* Archetype at the Conscious level is saying:

> *"Right! I'm sick of this old rubbish. I'm here to be my highest*

potential, remembering who I really am and get on with it.
I'm not going to let old fears or sabotage get in my way. So
let's go!"

It's so wonderful when the Child is at this level of Awareness, as it means you have a core strength within you that is ready to move mountains to create a whole new reality. It's best to utilize this force field straight away, as experience shows me that if you don't, it will begin to dissipate as old programs start to creep back in.

At the end of the day, it's a choice that is consciously made, while at the Unconscious level, you don't even know you've got a choice, as it's knee jerk reaction to the fear that consumes you.

WAKING UP

There are levels beyond the Symbolic of course as there are many different stages to Consciousness itself. Everything arises in Consciousness, but not everything is awake.

At the Symbolic level it may be likened to the Christ Consciousness. I'm told through different spiritual teachers that there are many levels beyond this, but they're not spoken about or understood until you live in them.

Here's a classic human example of the three different levels that I see happening all the time:

At the Unconscious or **Tribal** level, it appears like someone has betrayed or hurt you by their actions. Because of this hurt, you find yourself in the field of chaos and end up in the **Individuation** or Sub Conscious level feeling abandoned and betrayed, hurt, lost, rejected and alone. You dig deep within, find out where this hurt is really coming from (often your child-hood beliefs and experiences), feel it, own and integrate it, and then head off into the **Symbolic** or Conscious level.

It's from this vantage point you understand forgiveness, see it for what it is (an opportunity to move on from old ways of doing things), and begin to understand how this has all played out for your growth and the deeper purpose of waking up.

This is the basis of Carl Jung's work, who was a Swiss psychiatrist and founder of analytical psychology. His theories around the Collective Unconscious, including the concept of archetypes, underpin much of modern psychology today.

At the heart of analytical psychology is the understanding of the ego and here is where Jung's label of Individuation was developed. He believed that this understanding would lead to the Conscious or Symbolic level of the true self.

But this journey takes courage; it takes discipline and commitment to want to know the truth about who you really are. For a lot of people, they prefer to stay stuck in the drama of life, but for a few, they truly want to know, feel, and live as Love.

The majority of us on the earth plane are in a deep sleep, believing we are only the body, the five senses and our mind. Once we have our crises, or many of them, then we have the opportunity to join the ranks of those who realize that this is indeed a dream and want to wake up from this dream.

We start to realize that everything in the deep sleep state is based on pain and suffering and we desire to live differently to that, we desire to live as Sovereign Beings aware that we are all connected to each other through a deeper level of Consciousness. We truly desire to be free of the old mind and its fear based programs.

A good analogy here is when you go to sleep at night. You lose consciousness and move into the deep sleep states where you experience a completely different realm. This realm is totally real to you while you're in it, and for some, it's filled with angst, terror and fear and may even mean you wake up in a state of panic. At this point you heave a sigh of relief and say, "Thank goodness that was only a dream!"

Many wise sages throughout history liken our life on the earth plane to being in that dream state, to being asleep. It is totally real to us and we give it all our attention and our energy. But the wise Beings also tell us that it's a dream and we need to wake up from this dream to remember we're not the pain and suffering, we're not the separation from love, we're not the greed and power play. We've been seduced to believe this is true, but it's not.

If you're fully Conscious and Awake, then you march to the beat of your own drum, you live in the present moment, opening up the vastness of possibilities and potential. You totally follow the guidance from your own heart; you live as Love, give and receive it. At the same time, you look the same as everyone else, but radiate a deep sense of peace and harmony from within. No matter what is arising in the outside world, you remember the truth of your connection to your Heart/Spirit at all times. It never leaves you, as it is your only foundation.

You understand the play of your mind and don't buy into it. You honor your body for the vehicle it is, but you know it's not who you are, as it will drop away at some point and the eternal you will keep on existing. You no longer need addictions of any sort, you've dropped all beliefs and programmes you've inherited, and you're totally free to just BE. You experience great pockets of stillness, without thought going on, just Presence. There is enormous freedom in this state, as the old baggage can no longer bind you or cripple you.

What realm do *you* wish to live in? The deep sleep state perhaps the Awaking state or the fully Conscious state. Probably, like most of us, you move between all three levels, catching glimpses of the fully Conscious level but not able to fully live there yet.

7

CHALLENGING ARCHETYPES

Casting your own chart is a wonderful opportunity to see the game that is being played, to see the beliefs and thought forms that are blocking you, revealing your anxieties as well as your aspirations. It's a powerful blessing to be able to give this gift to yourself, to simply sit with what unfolds and feel into it, and actively work with these powerful insights.

Sometimes a chart may feel uncomfortable as it reveals a hidden aspect that is hard to own, but other times it will be a pat on the back that says you're on the right track. For me, all charts are wonderful because they present the truth and give me an opportunity to dig deeper and see what game I may be playing with myself, unconsciously.

Anyone can do this; it's easily explained in the next chapter how to cast your own chart. The only component that is needed is a desire to know a deeper truth.

For a complete understanding of the Archetypes I use in my readings, please go to Chapter Twelve. These Archetypes are explored at the Unconscious and Conscious levels. You may also view a full explanation of the entire Archetypes I use in video format if you go to my website:

www.archetypechartreadings.com

There are many different ways to look at Archetypes and lots of different labels and names, however I'm only talking about the ones that I personally use. You may wish to explore many other versions of them as well.

THE FOUR MAIN ARCHETYPES

In this map of the world, there are four main Archetypes that go in every single reading, because these four Archetypes will play out in your life until you take your last breath.

Other modalities will give you a different perspective on Archetypes, for example the Tarot. Their major Arcana are all based on twenty-two archetypal patterns. Carl Jung who popularized archetypes used other names such as The Hero, The Maiden and the Wise Old Man. Archetypes in fact go back to the days of Plato, and help us to frame and understand our experiences in life.

So let's look at this particular format, which I find works brilliantly.

The four main Archetypes are:

Child, **Victim**, **Prostitute** and **Saboteur.**

THE CHILD

The *Child* kicks in the moment you're born and you take on board a body. There are many variations to the *Child*, such as the Wounded Child, the Spoilt Child and the Entitled Child (which particularly plays out with Millennials). The Child Archetype denotes your level of maturity.

Marcel came to see me; he was born into a wealthy family situation. However, he had trouble holding onto relationships. The chart showed that his *Child* was still in his Tribal/Unconscious level and in fact, he'd never matured.

Marcel had trouble relating well to others, he was often very self absorbed and had trouble following things through to completion. He had a charisma about him, but he was so used to being pampered, he just expected life to go his way and was mystified when it didn't! The truth was, he had no idea how to grow up and become a man. You can be in your sixties or seventies, and still have your *Child* sitting at the Unconscious level.

THE VICTIM

The next one to arise is the *Victim*. This happens the moment you're not getting your needs met and may play out whenever you don't get your own way.

Tayla was a young lady who came for a Chart reading. Her *Victim* was very strong, as she felt life was too hard, she just wanted everything handed to her on a platter. Her parents had supported her brother with his professional career, but not Tayla who did not have the same aspirations. Her husband did not give her enough attention as he too was consumed by his career. Her friends were often too busy to see her. She had no idea that it was her attitude to life that turned people away as she just wanted to take everything but give very little. She wanted to be the center of attention at all times. This was her inner *Child* playing out, turning her into a *Victim*, as she felt like she always had to compete against her brother for attention. So Tayla felt that life was treating her unfairly as she wasn't getting the accolades she wanted.

THE PROSTITUTE

The next one confuses people because it's called the *Prostitute*. The *Prostitute* asks the following questions:

> *How are you out of your integrity? What are you doing to sell yourself short so that you can please others or gain something?*

Jill stayed in a loveless marriage because of the kudos she received. Things like the luxury car, unlimited access to as much money as she wanted, major trips overseas, in fact the epitome of the high life. But as Jill aged, she became miserable. The material world was starting to lose its glitter and this frightened her. Her deteriorating health was starting to show itself.

She knew she was prostituting herself but did not know how to stop doing it as her fear of not living the high life paralysed her. Jill was stuck in old beliefs that said the material world is the only thing that can make you happy.

THE SABOTEUR

The last one is the *Saboteur*. This Archetype arises every time you go to make change in your life, because that it's function. It will say things like:

"What if I make a fool of myself? What if I make a mistake?
Will I regret this and how much will it cost me?"

Greg knew this Archetype well. His lack of confidence was strong, and when he needed to make a career change, he sabotaged himself brilliantly by turning to drugs and getting high as a way of not dealing with his fear of change. He didn't care what job he did, so long as he was getting some money in.

He was actually highly intelligent but his childhood experiences meant he lacked self respect and had no sense of his own self worth. He had no idea he was sabotaging himself in this manner. He just saw it as "bad luck."

It was time to clear out old beliefs that were still running him. They certainly were not the truth but his inner *Child* and *Saboteur* were calling the shots, not the adult part of him.

Casting your own Chart will reveal where you sit with the four main archetypes of *Child, Victim, Prostitute* and *Saboteur*. Another eight will also come to the surface and all of this will present you with a picture of what's going on in your life right now.

I find it so helpful to see where the Archetype is sitting in the chart. If it's at a level that does not serve me, then this means I now have the knowledge and hopefully wisdom to turn it around so it is serving me. How to do this is discussed later on.

I'm hoping now that the statement "our biography becomes our biology," starts to make sense to you?

THREE WAYS WE ALL LOSE OUR ENERGY

There are three ways most of us lose our energy or vitality before we've even get out of bed in the morning.

Are you living constantly in the past?

One way is to the past, by being stuck in old thoughts and experiences – this is called the *Myth* Archetype. This happens when someone is holding onto regret, shame, bitterness, anger, vengeance, resentment or guilt. This can mean that this person is stuck in the past, needing to blame others or life for where they're at, or living constantly with sorrow and regret. Over the last forty years, I've seen this old thinking lead to all sorts of bowel issues, for example Irritable Bowel Syndrome, as well as all sorts of bowel cancers, Crones Disease and/or heart issues.

I've found that there are some cultures that excel in living in the past, by carrying the wounds of their tribe or family and forcing it onto new generations. Some children carry the beliefs of their parents so strongly that they grow up hating people they've never even met. This is happening in our world right now. Have you noticed this?

I remember a young man in his twenties, Ashley, teaching a group of Prep students at a very multicultural school. He said they all got on so well, holding hands, sharing with each other or playing games outside in their lunch break.

But by the time they were in Grade Three, these same children were in groups, fighting with each other, calling each other names, and totally split into their cultural differences and beliefs. This was not taught to them by the school system, it came from the home, their religion and culture. This is the

Myth at the lowest Unconscious level. The good news is that at the Conscious level you learn how to let go of your past, as you bring forth another perspective and learn how to exercise forgiveness and move on.

Chelsea was a young woman who had experienced a lifetime of being put down by males. Her father was abusive and so was her husband. Chelsea was repeating an old pattern by marrying the same sort of man. Chelsea became ill with bowel cancer, so her chart showed she was hanging onto huge resentment to her father and husband. She was frightened to speak her truth to either of these males, or indeed all males.

Gradually over time she became empowered. Chelsea learned how to make her own decisions, as she came from a place of self-love, learning how to trust in her own inner guidance and eventually stood up to these bullies and became well again. Even though the marriage didn't last, Chelsea gained a whole new perspective as she dealt with all levels of her illness, physically, emotionally, mentally, and spiritually. Not everyone can do this, but Chelsea had the courage to do the work and move on.

Derek too came from an abusive background, physically, emotionally and mentally. His parents gave him little attention, as they were caught up in their alcoholic world. It was no surprise to hear that he had married someone who was only available to him on a superficial level, as his parents had been.

Derek was just repeating an old pattern, in effect recreating his childhood. Derek drew *Knight/Father/Sage*, which shows you the journey through the different stages of masculinity. It refers to the young adult stage, then the fathering component and finally, hopefully, the wisdom that comes with learning from our experiences. It was time for Derek to claim his wisdom and turn his life around.

Over time, the stress of being "on guard" exhausted his adrenals, and the unconscious belief that said "I'm not safe to trust life" took its toll. He had a major heart attack, but Derek was ready to do the work required to call his power back from his wounded past and get on with his life.

This is scary work for most men as it means feeling the feelings they've usually denied, but with support and encouragement, Derek went on to create a whole new life for himself.

Do you get lost in the Future?

The second way we can lose our energy is to the future through the *Worrier* Archetype. This is an Archetype that nearly everyone can relate to as we're shown and taught that worry is a natural thing and we all do it. However, what worry really means is that you're sending your fears for someone or something out into the Universe and most specifically, into the future. If you think about it, you can only worry about something that hasn't happened yet.

In effect you're saying I don't trust life, so I'll do fear instead, which means worry. For many people, they see worry as a way of being caring and concerned, which of course, is a learned belief system they've inherited from somewhere.

We've become so acclimatised to worry, that we don't give it another thought as we see it as the norm. We all do it, and we don't even realize that it's harmful to ourselves.

Worry is energy or fear based thinking. It logs in at the cellular level and at some point in the future, can make you ill. You cannot worry and do trust at the same time. They are in different ballparks. So at some point, we have to make a choice.

For example, I know one mother Cindy, who had to learn the hard way about worry when her son did a big drug trip for ten years. When we did charts together, she often pulled the *Worrier*. Cindy realized that by worrying about her son, she was only adding more fear-based negativity to the situation.

Instead I taught her how to hold a vision of her son being well, strong, healthy, listening to his heart, following his intuition, walking his walk, being in his integrity and following his creativity and passion. Cindy took this on board and became very aware of her thinking and how much she worried automatically. She chose consciously each time to not go there and instead did what was suggested.

Cindy got through this troubling time and learned how to use her mind constructively instead of destructively. A nice touch is the fact that her son got through his drug experience and went on to become a wonderful young man.

Worrying only harms the self. Our mind does not know we're worrying about another person or situation. It only understands the energy of worry, which is another name for fear. It logs into your system to create stress, which then translates as illness at some point.

Ironically, you need a role model to teach you how to worry because of your own volition you actually don't know how to do it. So usually, one of your parents will instil this unwanted vice into your energy field.

A child picks up on worry and stress instinctively. If you're saying to your child: "It's good, it's all fine, Mummy and Daddy are ok," and it's not the truth, the child will know at an instinctual level that this is a lie. It knows you're not in your integrity and that translates to the child as "I'm not safe." So worrying is a learned behavior.

Helen was so addicted to worry that she obsessed over everything. It was a huge issue for her and literally created different Obsessive Compulsive Disorders in her life and at one point, it even manifested as brain tumors, which thankfully turned out to be benign. Needless to say, she often pulled the *Worrier!* She saw it as part of her world and that everyone did it, so therefore it was not an issue. She had learned how to worry from her mother.

Gradually Helen came to understand it was harming her, in many different ways. She too was teaching this to her daughters so it was becoming generational. Helen could not imagine her life without worry as she was so identified with it. But with help and understanding, she improved and moved on.

Many illnesses come out of worry, or a popular label these days is to call it stress. The media tells you at the sub conscious level to worry, because of all its fear-based stories about what's happening in the world. It is constantly giving you a message to live in fear for your future, be it your health, terrorism, your job or financial security. It's a vicious circle and one we would do well to unlearn. There are ways that can help you to let go of worry, as it's a major addiction on the planet.

Difficulty being in the Present?

The third way we can lose our energy field is the *Judge* Archetype in present time and space. I've already mentioned the *Judge* several times, as being caught up in good/bad or right/wrong. Ironically, you have to judge something to worry about it so the *Judge* and *Worrier* Archetypes are inextricably linked.

Judgment separates us out from our heart as the energy of judgment stays in the body and taps into the ego/mind as "I'm better than you," or I'm less than you," depending on the circumstances.

Judgment kicks into the *Controller* as well. I remember one man, Archie, who was used to being in a powerful position at work. The time came when Archie had to retire as he was in his mid sixties and the company replaced him with a bright young man. Archie felt lost and devastated about this change of direction, though he put on a brave face.

About a year after retiring Archie was diagnosed with Prostate Cancer. When we did his chart, it became obvious that he was furious about being forced to retire as his whole identity was caught up in his job, his power and his financial position. He felt that his life no longer had any meaning. He was strongly judging the situation and felt out of control, as it was not what he wanted.

He found it impossible to consider other alternatives as he was very work oriented and nothing else had any appeal to him. He had totally put all his eggs into the one basket.

Unfortunately, life doesn't always work out the way we want it to.

So these three Archetypes of *Myth, Judge and Worrier* may all lead to debilitating illnesses of some sort. Most of us leak our power to one of these three, if not all of these three, which means we've lost seventy-five percent of our energy field before we even get out of bed in the morning. Then we wonder why we're exhausted all the time. It's because we're not present.

We're either in the past, or the future, or if we are in the here and now, we're too busy judging it.

FOLLY ARCHETYPES

Fantasy Archetype

Some of the Archetypes appear as benign, but actually, at the Unconscious or Tribal level, they're quite dangerous. One that comes to mind is the *Fantasy* Archetype. This Archetype, when it appears at the lower level, means that the person is not "here," as they're not present or grounded and definitely not in their body.

Let me explain what I mean by "not in their body."

Cathie's father abused her sexually. When any form of physical abuse takes place, the child learns very quickly that the body is not a safe place to be. So this is where the *Fantasy* kicks in. Cathie learned how to live in her imagination, not eat very well, she was vague and had trouble making decisions. She simply was not safe to be here, so lived in the mental realms all the time. This of course can become dangerous as the adult. Especially if you do things like driving a car, because you live in your own little world and do not pay attention to traffic lights or other signals.

It was difficult for Cathie to perform at work, or to be responsible for her decision-making and to show up on time to appointments. She had to learn how to establish a different relationship to her body, to feel safe to be in it as the adult. As Cathie became more conscious, she could see her childhood from another perspective and therefore move into more joy and trust from within.

Over time, we can learn the power of forgiveness and hopefully learn how to understand we're all capable of being the Archetype of the Saint and equally, we're all capable of being the Archetype of the "Devil," which is our shadow side.

Thankfully, most of us choose not play out the extreme of the Shadow, but, as is obvious, some people do make this choice. However, it serves all of us to address our Shadow side and get to know it well, without judgment. It's all part of the human experience.

Is the *Fantasy* Archetype playing out in your life?

Do you often find yourself day dreaming a lot? Is it hard for you to stay focused, or pay attention to what others are saying to you? Do you get speeding fines because you're not paying attention? Is it hard for you to be fully present, in your body, on a daily basis? There are many reasons behind this, so maybe it's time to explore a bit more.

Caretaker Archetype

Another Archetype that springs to mind is the *Caretaker*. This innocuous sounding Archetype is self-explanatory, however, it's actually dangerous at the Unconscious level. Why? Because behind the *Caretaker* sits a belief that you're only valid if you're taking care of others.

Jane came to see me after her breast cancer experience. When I did Jane's chart, it was clear that she had the classic *Caretaker* playing out in a huge way. She was the oldest female of ten siblings, then she had ten children herself, and when I saw her, she was looking after all the grandchildren. I remember saying to her that if she could write the script what would it look like?

Jane said, "That's easy. I would just paint all day." So I pretended to write her a prescription to do exactly that. The grandchildren were not her responsibility, but out of an addiction to taking care of others, she just did it.

It was great to hear that years later she was still healthy as she painted herself into wellness! She started taking care of her own needs instead of putting others first.

Do you tend to put other peoples needs before your own? Do you feel guilty if you have to say NO to requests with friends or maybe at work? Is it hard for you to do kind things for yourself so you put off doing them completely? Where is the *Caretaker* in your life?

Martyr Archetype

The *Martyr* is in a similar vein. Martyrs have no idea how to live their own life, or express their own creativity and passion; instead they usually do it through others. As is the case with the *Worrier*, you need a role model to become a *Martyr*, and this too will usually be given to you by one of your parents. *Martyrs* often sigh a lot. Behind the sigh is the unspoken language that says: "If you only knew how much I'm sacrificing for your sake. One day you may perhaps pay me back for all that I'm doing for you."

The *Martyr* at the lower level does not recognize that it's a choice, yet the reality is that it's an addiction and an excuse for choosing not to live a joyful life. Instead, they may live vicariously through others. I learned this pattern well from both of my parents and it needed a lot of awareness to change it all around, especially when it's mixed with the *Surrogate* and *Workaholic* Archetypes. It's insidious how subtle these patterns can be and we're not aware of them in the slightest. Until we get a wake up call that is!

Do you sigh a lot? Often we don't even know we're doing it so sometimes we have to ask others if they notice this trend in us. Do you find yourself putting up with a lot of pain, be it physical, mental or emotional?How do you feel about giving yourself joy or pursuing a passion?

Is the *Martyr* in your life? Perhaps you can see this pattern in one of your parents, or maybe both? Have you inherited it too?

Perfectionist Archetype

Let's look at the *Perfectionist* as I see it regularly playing out in people's charts. When we feel unsafe as a child, we unconsciously look around for roles to play that will keep us loved, approved of and therefore "safe." This is where the *Perfectionist* comes in.

The rationale, at the Unconscious level says that if I'm perfect at everything I do, then I'll always be safe, receive accolades and everything will be fine and of course "perfect." It's exhausting having to be perfect all the time. It leads to many illnesses, mostly stress based, such as ulcers, migraines, skin conditions, eye sight issues or throat conditions to name a few.

I know many clients who have had crippling migraines because of the *Perfectionist* within. Hopefully, eventually, you'll wake you up that it's a waste of time and not possible anyway. There is no such thing as perfection on this planet, it's all perfectly imperfect. No such thing as the perfect child, the perfect job, the perfect relationship, the perfect parent, yet so many of us strive for this. It's only the ego/mind that makes you believe this is possible, not the heart.

Do you strive to be "perfect" at nearly everything you do? Is it necessary for your home/office/wardrobe/work space to always be in top order otherwise you can't function? Do you beat yourself up if you believe you've failed in some way? How about comparing yourself to others?

The *Perfectionist* is alive and well in so many of us. For some of us it's dominant in the work place, but for others, it plays out more at home. If it really has hold of you, it will be across the board.

Perhaps it's time to look at the motivation behind being the *Perfectionist* and go within to see if it serves you. It can be changed, but first it has to be owned.

Fool's Love Archetype

Another Archetype worth mentioning is *Fool's Love*. At the Unconscious level, it plays out in a few different ways.

Lisa came for a chart reading as she'd had many different intimate relationships over the years but none of them worked out. They lasted a couple of years, but then they eventually died. It was a strong pattern for her. Needless to say, all Lisa wanted was to feel loved by another, feel safe and honored in the intimacy, hopefully have children and a family life. This does not seem too much to ask, as it's most people's desire to have this at some point in their lives.

Lisa's pattern was to drop quickly into a relationship with anyone who looked slightly interested in her. She did not have clear boundaries and there was an air of desperation around her. Her biological clock was ticking and so it was her dream to get married and have children.

What Lisa usually did was to give herself sexually very quickly so as to "secure" the relationship, then in her mind, create all sorts of expectations as to what will happen in the future with this new person. She was not present as most of her energy lay in the future around what she wanted to happen. This is very common with a lot of females. After a short while, Lisa's neediness and criticism of her new partner kicked in and all Lisa could see was that he wasn't giving her what she wanted. At the Unconscious level we need to blame the other person for everything that goes wrong.

Another level of *Fool's Love* is the person who becomes the doormat as they give so much of themselves. Behind this scenario lies the belief that one day, I'll start to receive it all back and the relationship will move onto an equal footing of giving and receiving. Unfortunately, this doesn't happen as there's no self-love present and at the Unconscious level, it stays this way until the person wakes up that it's not fulfilling living this way. Thankfully these patterns or roles can change, but it does take growing up or becoming Conscious to bring about the changes.

We're all energetic Beings and what you believe is what you create. If only we knew how to fall so deeply and completely in love with ourselves, (not narcissistically), then the energy of real love is what we would give out. Not needy love, not doormat love, not pseudo empty love, or Disneyland love - but real love! Sadly, for most of us, we lack roles models for this and our beliefs and attitudes to love are formed in our childhood.

Unless we get a loving example of intimacy, then we won't

know how to live like this. What makes it worse in the modern age, is how children are brought up with screens as their companions. I've watched teenagers at parties. Half of them spend their time texting other friends rather than engaging in real face-to-face conversation. They don't know how to mix with strangers let alone talk to them, so they hide behind their screens. It's possible that real conversation may die out completely one day.

The answer to *Fool's Love* is, if you can feel real love for yourself; where you honor yourself; respect your own boundaries; know the balance in resting, playing and working; and you get to fill your creative needs; then you have the opportunity to come into wholeness and harmony.

If you can also manage to bring fun into your life, and have a handle on money, as well as take responsibility for your own growth, then this is the sort of person you will attract into your life. You cannot manifest into your reality that which is not your inner truth. It's not a match.

What was your role model for love in your childhood? Was it uplifting and heart based, or was it filled with angst, mixed messages, even violence of any type?

Do you find it easy to hold conversations with people you don't know really well? How difficult is it for you to be out and about socially, genuinely enjoying yourself and not hide behind a mobile screen?

Drama Queen Archetype

The last Archetype I will mention is the *Drama Queen*. This plays out a lot with teenage girls and other sections of the community. It is exhausting playing this role (as it is with many of the Archetypes at the Unconscious level). You have to create drama of some sort in your life, to feel involved, to be liked and noticed and if you don't have enough drama of your own, you will borrow other people's and get caught up in it.

It may be that you become obsessed with TV stars or so called "reality" shows. The *Drama Queen* is classic avoidance of deeply looking at yourself, your beliefs and patterns, and instead you become addicted to drama of your own making or involving someone else.

Adele had a tough upbringing. She was deserted by her parents at an early age, carved out a career for herself, had two children and did an amazing job bringing up those children on her own. Adele provided a house for them, which gave them some level of security, which she herself had never known. But there was always drama in Adele's life. The dramas were so numerous that I couldn't even begin to detail them all.

Unknowingly, it was a strong addictive, behavioral pattern that was so prominent in her life, she didn't know any other way of living. It created health issues, plus relationship issues with many people who ran the *Rescuer*. I constantly saw Adele being hurt by others as indeed she hurt others too. She had no idea how to trust people or even let them in. This was a case where working with her did not make a difference to her pattern and choices. The pattern was so strong and so addictive and the repercussions of this behavior so debilitating, that pain and suffering just continued on.

The way through for the *Drama Queen* is to recognize the programing and patterning, to find Self Love within and learn how to trust. This is the work of a lifetime. It helps to have someone guide you, but hopefully, at some point, the light bulb will switch on and the unfolding of the old patterns can leave. Then new ones, couched in love, can take their place.

Have you ever played the *Drama Queen*? Did you enjoy it? What was the pay off? Excitement, feeling included, always having someone or something to gossip about? On reflection, was this kind and caring? Do you still do this? Are you ready to move on?

All of the above examples can be turned around. Nothing is fixed and change is always possible. We need to look at the maturation of our motivation. Is our behavior based on past patterning? Does it mean that our inner Child is controlling our thinking, coming from a place of fear? Are we ready to choose a heart response instead?

So now that you've learned a bit about the Archetypes, as roles and patterns in our lives, let's play with them a bit more.

SO LET'S PLAY!

CASTING YOUR FIRST CHART

Let's do something exciting and cast a chart for yourself. There are so many benefits from casting a chart, as it's about self-understanding and self-knowledge and may provide clues with regard to helping you shift old patterns.

People often ask me, "How often do I cast a chart for myself?" There is no set rule, so my response is "When your intuition tells you to do so." It may be once a year, or every few months. Perhaps your circumstances change and you're unsure of which direction to go, so a chart at this particular time may be very opportune.

I'm always keen to see where my Tribal/Unconscious Archetypes are sitting because they are the ones that help me see where old beliefs and ways of doing things are sitting.

The Tribal Archetypes are always the gift in my humble opinion. The Symbolic ones say "well done, you've got a handle on this." The Tribals say "pay attention and look into this further."

You will already know this on some deep level of your Being. However, the Charts bring it to the surface and into your Awareness. What a blessing this is. This skill is now at your fingertips so let's get going.

A detailed knowledge about all of the Archetypes sits at the back of this book in Chapter Twelve. So does the information about the Astrological Houses, in Chapter Eleven. You do not need to know about astrological Planets and Signs, only the Houses. To interpret your chart, you will need to refer to these chapters so that the chart makes sense to you.

There are two ways to cast a chart:

1. You may purchase a pack of archetype cards by going to my website and ordering them online. This set of cards includes all the Archetypes, plus the twelve houses of the Astrological Wheel and the three Levels of Consciousness. (www. archetypechartreadings.com)

2. You may decide to be totally playful and creative by making your own cards of the Archetypes, the twelve Houses and the three Levels.

Feel free to add or make up any other Archetypes that appeal to you. There are many that I don't have or use, but I do find, after having done so many charts, that the existing ones cover all aspects of life's challenges.

Next, you can also make up your own Astrological wheel and the Internet has many examples of how to do this. Or you can download it for free from my website and print it out for this exercise. It looks like this:

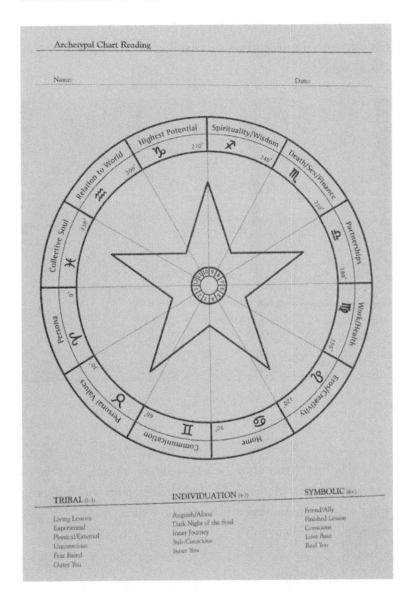

TRIBAL (1-3)

Living Lessons
Experiential
Physical/External
Unconscious
Fear Based
Outer You

INDIVIDUATION (4-7)

Anguish/Alone
Dark Night of the Soul
Inner Journey
Sub-Conscious
Inner You

SYMBOLIC (8+)

Friend/Ally
Finished Lesson
Conscious
Love Base
Real You

So let's assume you have the Archetypes in front of you, (using either your own creative pack or mine).

You have the Astrological Wheel printed out, and you have the twelve cards representing the astrological houses (numbered one to twelve).

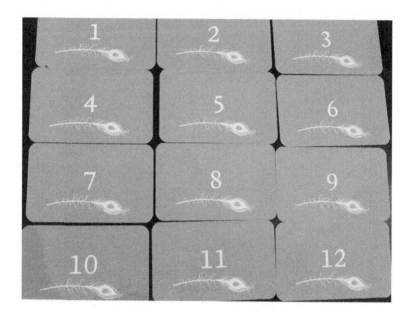

You also have the three cards relating to the Levels of Consciousness, with the words Tribal written on one, Individuation written on another and Symbolic written on the last one. Now you're ready to go!

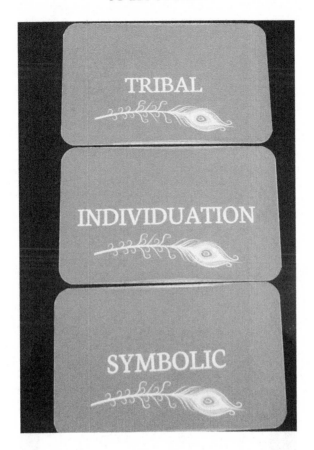

There are four main Archetypes that you will use every time you do a reading. These four will play out continuously in your life until you die or have become totally Conscious. I have discussed them briefly in Chapter Seven, but they are: *Child, Victim, Prostitute and Saboteur.*

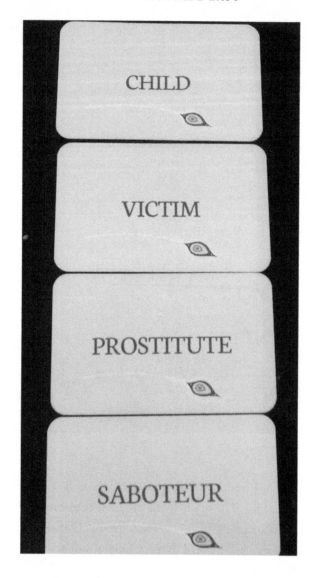

It's helpful to always separate out the four main Archetypes from the bulk of the pack, as you'll use them over and over again. This saves you time having to hunt through the pack whenever you want to do a chart reading.

Next, lay out the rest of the Archetypes face down on a table. If you have my cards, then just fanning them out in front of you works well, but if you've made your own, then you may have to just place them all face down in front of you. You should not be able to see the name of the Archetype.

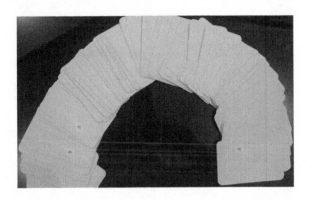

Easy steps to follow:

Take a deep breath, center yourself somehow, clear your mind, only being focused on yourself and ask the following question:

"What do I need to know right now that is for my highest good?"

Then take the following steps:

- Choose eight Archetypes from the cards, not knowing what you've chosen at this point.

- Add the four main Archetypes of *Child, Victim,*
  Prostitute and Saboteur to give you twelve cards.

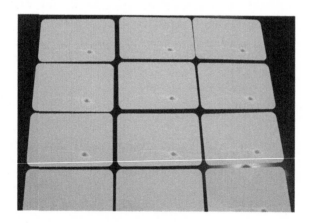

Now you have twelve Archetypes in front of you, four you
already know and eight you don't, but they're all lying face
down on the table so you can't see any labels at all.

Next take the cards of the twelve houses of the Astrological Wheel, turn them upside down so you can't see the number of the house and pair them up, So take one Archetype card and pair it with one of the cards from the Astrological Wheel. You do this twelve times in total, so you end up with twelve pairs of cards, each one containing one Archetype and one card, numbered one to twelve which represents one of the houses of the Wheel.

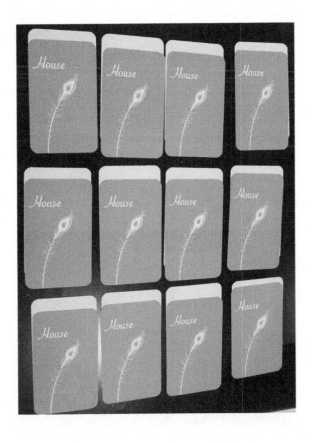

- The next part is the tricky bit. You have only three cards left, with the label Tribal (or Unconscious), Individuation (or Sub-Conscious) and Symbolic (or

Conscious). It's now time to make a pledge of honor. Pledge to be as open and honest with yourself as possible. Pledge to want to know your own deepest truth.

You only have three cards to choose from so it's easy to remember what is where, but if you seriously and genuinely want to know where you're at, then you'll mix them up each time so that you can't remember which card is what. My rationale behind this is why play games about the truth, life is too short and personally speaking, I want to be the most Conscious ME I can be, so I want the truth.

- Turning these three cards upside down so you can't see the label, shuffle them around so you can't remember what is where, then choose one of these three cards and place it on top of one of the pairs (Archetype and House).

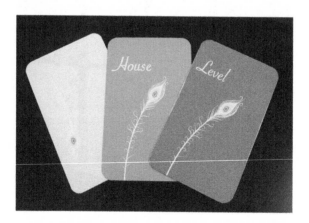

- Now turn it over and look at what you have in front of you. As an example, it may read Victim, the number two and Symbolic (or Conscious). Now get the

printed form of the astrological wheel and write in the
second house the word Victim and the word Symbolic
or Conscious or perhaps just use an initial, S or C.
This will tell you that in the second house you have
the Archetype of the Victim and it's at the Symbolic
level.

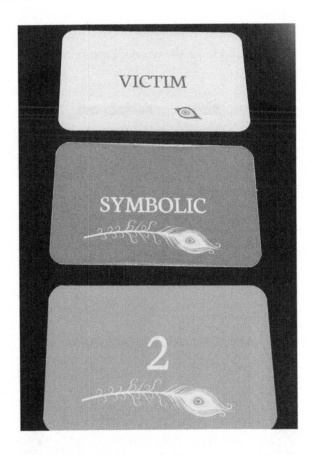

- Put the Victim Archetype card aside, put the House
  number card aside and return to your three levels of
  Consciousness. Turn them upside down again; shuffle
  them around so you can't remember what is where
  and then choose one of these three cards again.

- Having chosen another card from the Levels, now place it on top of the next pair (Archetype and House). Do the same thing again, turn the three cards up and see what they say. For example, they may read Caretaker, house number seven, Tribal (or Unconscious).

- Take your printed astrological wheel again and write in the seventh House the word Caretaker and the letter T or U.

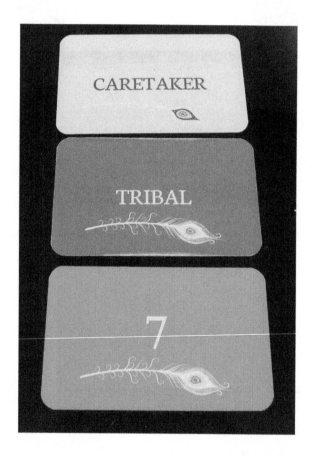

- Then place the Archetype of the Caretaker aside in the general pack. Place the House aside also. I usually put the houses all together and the Archetypes all together, but I keep the main four separate from all the other Archetypes so it's easy to find them next time I do a chart.

- Place the blue Level card back in with the other two cards, turn them upside down so you can't see the word written on the Level and shuffle again.

- Repeat this process twelve times in total, until the entire Wheel is filled in with an Archetype and a Level of Consciousness. Well done. You've just drawn up your first Archetype Chart Reading.

NOW FOR THE EXPLANATION

Until you're used to this format, it will mean going to the back of the book and checking out the Archetype and writing out its meaning. Then you'll have to go to the relevant house that the Archetype is sitting in.

If you downloaded my free Astrological Wheel, you will see a few brief words that give clues to the House, but a deeper explanation is contained in Chapter Eleven.

Once you've written it all out, or recorded it, then you will start to get an understanding of what the Chart wants to tell you.

I won't lie to you; there is a definite skill in being able to pull a Chart together. It takes practice to harness this skill, but this is no different to any other skill you've learned along the way. It may help to go to my website to look at the videos I've done on different Chart Readings:

www.archetypechartreadings.com

Remember the first time you drove a manual car? It wasn't easy co-ordinating the indicators, the brake, the accelerator, the rear view mirror and the gear stick. The Archetype charts are no different. It takes effort to become good at this.

Polarities

I often work in Polarities or what is called an Opposition. So this means I look at the First house, then move across to the Seventh house, it's opposite. I will do the same with the Second house, being opposite the Eighth, then Third house opposite the Ninth, and so on. It just depends what stands out to me.

The reason I do this is because where the Archetype sits in a house tells you how it's relating to your world. What is opposite it (or in Polarity) is very impactful and influences the Archetype.

For example, if you had *Perfectionist* in the First House at Tribal and it was opposite the *Slave* in the Seventh House at Tribal, this would suggest that needing to be perfect all the time, at everything you do, is an addiction that consumes you. It's how you look to the outside world (First House) and it's a strong belief inside of you that says I won't be safe unless I'm perfect at everything (Seventh House). This belief may lead to huge stress in your life and eventually illness.

Sometimes there are all Symbolics on the bottom of the chart and all Tribals on the top. To have lots of Symbolic Archetypes on the bottom of the Chart means that you're on track, you have a good understanding of what is going on in your life, especially your physical world and can shift or work with things that are not going well for you.

Conversely, to have lots of Tribals in the upper part of the Chart can mean that there are old beliefs that no longer serve you, especially with regard to your spiritual or inner world and it would be helpful to address this.

It can also mean that you're at new beginnings and the fear of walking a new pathway is very strong within.

I remember when it came time to sell Jamieson Sanctuary. I had worked so hard to earn the money to build this place, to market it and establish it that when it came time to leave (as guided by Spirit) I felt very fearful. I had no idea where I was going or what I would do with myself.

My marriage had broken down and I was feeling very alone. I did a chart reading for myself and it reflected this perfectly. I had ten Archetypes at the Tribal level. This of course, was totally appropriate as I was fearful of leaving everything I had worked so hard to create.

It was interesting for me to cast Charts every four to six months as they totally reflected my journey and my progress. Would you do this for yourself, or is it too scary to explore your inner world?

Other times, in Chart readings, there's a component of Symbolics opposite Tribals. This usually means that doubting mind is having a field day within. One part of you, perhaps your heart is saying, "Go on, you can do this." But another part, usually the mind, is saying, "Stay safe and don't rock the boat!" This internal yo-yo back and forth can drive you up the wall.

Sometimes the chart is nearly all Tribal and only one or two Symbolics. As before, it can mean you're dominated by fear based thinking at the moment or it can mean it's time to walk a whole new pathway in life.

They all mean different things depending on what Archetype is sitting where and at what level. The whole Chart needs to be viewed in its entirety, though it helps to tease out certain aspects that stand out to you. Perhaps there's a pattern, but maybe there isn't.

I have never, ever seen someone have a chart with all Symbolics! That's the level of the evolved soul. What we tend to do is have a mixture. If you have a lot at the Symbolic level, it does not mean that you're the wisest Being on the planet and can sit back and put your feet up. It says that you're getting close to finishing off this particular part of your journey.

Lots of Symbolic's says you're about to graduate, but it doesn't say what from? It may be pre-school for all you know. On the other hand, if you have only one at the Symbolic level, may mean you're about to submit your Thesis for your PhD and therefore embark on new beginnings.

How many you have at Tribal or Symbolic typically does not say a lot about your wisdom or spiritual knowledge. It is talking about where you're blocked right now and gives you clues as to how to shift this block.

An example of this would be if you had all the following Archetypes at the Tribal level: *Victim, Prostitute, Philosopher, Square Peg in a Round Hole* and *Mystic*.

These Archetypes may be saying that the block is around the fear of following your own instincts. The fear is of being different, of standing out and taking a new direction in life.

You may be selling yourself short by listening to your mind all the time. The Chart may instead suggest you need to be more creative and open up to your right brain or listen to your heart's wisdom. You may be running old thoughts that tell you you're not good enough to change direction or what will others think if you do? This to me is empowering to understand, as it then gives you an opportunity to change these old thought patterns.

I find the Tribals are really the gifts in a reading. The Symbolic level says you have a handle on this part of your life for the moment. The Tribal level says there's something going on for you at the Unconscious level that is hidden from you.

This is the reason I've included a sample question at the Tribal or Unconscious Level (in the full explanation of the Archetypes), as it's a place to start challenging yourself on what it is that you're hiding from yourself.

You are a powerful person, a wondrous Creator, but you may have forgotten this. There isn't anything that you can't change. You just have to know about it, so that you can do something about it.

This doesn't mean to say that you will make a change; it just says you now have an opportunity to bring about change if you choose to do so. Life is always a choice.

Any Archetype that sits at the Individuation level is saying that you are stuck at the cross roads in your life. Spirit or your Higher Self is saying to you "Let's make a change, let's walk a new pathway as the old one doesn't serve you any more."

But you're standing at the crossroads replying, "Please give me the guarantee that I can't mess up, make a fool of myself or lose anything if I take the new pathway?" You're bargaining internally before you'll walk a new pathway. However, Spirit doesn't work this way as it knows fear is the illusion.

It can also mean that you're running old thoughts that no longer serve you. Again, your Higher Self wants you to throw out old thinking and get a different set of values, attitudes and perceptions. Hopefully, you'll start getting in touch with your heart's highest truth.

If this is something that resonates with you and you'd like to learn more about it, then go to my website (www.archetype-chartreadings.com), join up and there you'll see many video examples of how to do a reading for someone.

If you haven't the time or inclination to do any of the above, but still wish to experience a reading, you can book a chart reading, choose your cards and we'll explore it together.

9

EXAMPLE OF A CHART READING

In this chapter I'm going to walk you through an example of a chart reading. We will be using Melanie's chart to explore the polarities. It may be tempting to skip this chapter, but the best way to get better at doing your own or other people's charts, is through seeing charts in action. I will talk you through it, the same way I would a real client. Step by step, you will be better able to understand how to interpret charts.

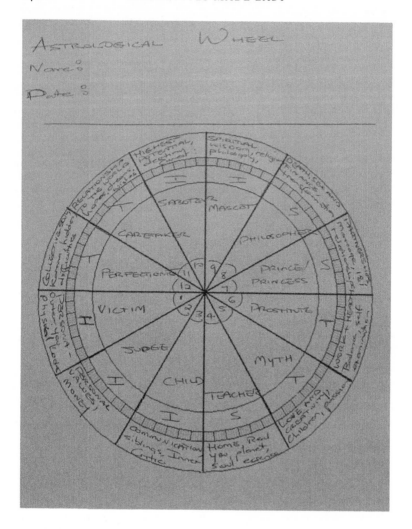

FIRST HOUSE

How you project to the Outside World

Melanie has *Victim* at the Individuation or Sub Conscious level. There's something that Melanie is thinking that is turning her into a Victim. It's not obvious to the outside world, as it's an inner reality at the Individuation level, but it's where she is at right now.

It could mean that Melanie is thinking that life is too hard, it's always a struggle or she's not getting anywhere. Perhaps she still believes in childhood messages that say she's not enough is some way, too loud or too demanding.

Anything at the Individuation level (or inner realms) means you're running old thoughts that no longer serve you, plus you're at a cross roads in your life.

So for Melanie, there is an old level of thinking that she is perpetuating that no longer serves her. What this thinking is, will unfold with the rest of the chart. She is at the cross roads because her Higher Self is waving a flag in her direction and saying, "Please examine what you're doing."

Even though this First House is the Outer You or the face you show to the world, archetypally it's saying that where Melanie is at right now, the old thoughts she's running are not helping her. This old thinking is part of a program she's inherited in her childhood. By holding onto it, she is victimizing herself and not moving forward.

Let's now take a look at the Seventh House.

SEVENTH HOUSE

Partnerships

Melanie has *Prince/Princess* at the Symbolic or Conscious level, the wisest part of herself. Anything at the Symbolic level is wonderful because it means that you've earned your "brownie points" to get there by walking through the Individuation level of chaos and madness!

We'd all love to avoid the Inner level or the sub conscious realm, as it makes us feel uncomfortable, but we can't. In ancient terms, it's called your "right of passage." To get to the Symbolic level or wise part of ourselves, we have to live the experience, not just read about it or think about it. This is true in all cultures and from all walks of life.

What this means is that Melanie has the ability to shift this old thinking that is victimizing her. She is willing to do the work, roll her sleeves up and get going. It means she is willing to listen to her Higher Self's guidance. This is the House of significant One on One relationships, be it to friends, colleagues, family, partner, workmates, and her peer group. However, the most significant one on one relationship is to herself and through to her Higher Self.

Prince/Princess also represents the duality within of the masculine/feminine principle. Melanie is able to listen to this wise part within (that sits at her heart) and allow this part to guide her. She can, if she so chooses, fall into Union within herself. Melanie can allow the heart to guide her, bring the left brain/right brain into harmony or the inner masculine/feminine components into equality.

Let's now explore the Second House.

SECOND HOUSE

Personal Values and Money

Melanie has *Judge* at the Individuation or inner level. This is the house that stores your belief systems around money, what you've learned from your parents, culture, religion, education system and the media about the value of money.

It also represents the Inner You and how you feel about yourself on the inside. It's the hidden part that only your closest friend or partner may know about you. This house is about self worth, self-esteem and self-respect.

There are three core beliefs that sit in this house – not being good enough, what will other people think, and the need for approval. If anything is Tribal in this house, it's saying that work needs to be done to shift these old beliefs, which usually come from your childhood programs.

However, because Melanie has this at the Individuation level, it's saying that *sometimes* she still judges herself with regard to not feeling good enough, or perhaps she still worries about what others may think or still needs approval from some people in her life. It's not major in her life, but minor.

She may hide this from the outside world, because this is the Second house, the inner part of herself. It's the fact that it's the *Judge* Archetype that gives you the clue that it's not so much about money but it's way more about her values. *Prince/Princess* in the Seventh house is saying that she may be able to shift this old behavior, because it's Symbolic and ready to be integrated now.

Let's now move to the Eighth House.

EIGHTH HOUSE

Sex, Death and Finance

The Archetype here is the *Philosopher* at the Symbolic or

Conscious level. This means that Melanie has the ability to transform (as it is the house of transformation) into her higher mind or the wise part of herself. The human mind is full of judgment at the Tribal level but here it means Melanie can tap into her own profound wisdom if she chooses to.

Coupled with *Prince/Princess* in the Seventh house, this says that it is possible for Melanie now to do the work she needs to, let go of old belief systems, and shift to a higher way of thinking. It means she is willing to let her Higher Self guide her and move from old mind at the Tribal level, to higher mind at the Symbolic level.

But first she has to let go of her *Judge* Archetype, either judgment of self or others, spoken or unspoken. Judgment separates her out from her heart's highest truth. Instead, Melanie needs to focus on discernment.

We're onto the Third House.

THIRD HOUSE

Communication

Melanie has *Child* at the Individuation or Sub Conscious level. This means that she has to watch her inner critic, her judgmental thoughts, perhaps how she talks to herself or her constant mind chatter.

It's akin to saying that the child within has run me long enough. It's now time to become the adult. Melanie needs to take her power back from old ways of communicating with others and with herself.

The *Child* Archetype at this level is saying, "Can I/can't I, will

I/won't I, should I/shouldn't I make this necessary shift from old ways of doing things to a higher way of looking at my life?"

Remember that the Child's biggest fear is of the unknown. This means that the Child within would rather stay in a comfort zone, even though it's an uncomfortable place to be, as opposed to moving out into the world of the unknown.

Let's now move to the Ninth House.

NINTH HOUSE

Spirituality/Wisdom

Melanie has *Mascot* at the Individuation or Sub Conscious level. This means that sometimes Melanie knows who she is and at other times she has no idea, or is too scared to be who she wants to be.

This may mean that deep down she knows that she needs to listen to her Higher Self more and follow her own wisdom, but she's so used to playing the roles that others want her to play. There's a fear still running her (coming from her Child) that says, "Stay safe, stay safe, don't rock the boat too much or it will mean a scary ride!"

The Mascot is like a Chameleon; it changes shape or behaviors according to who it is with at the time, to stay safe and not cause upheaval.

There's a part of Melanie that knows she needs to take more time out to listen within, have some more stillness in her life, but her *Child* in the Third house will be pushing her towards keeping busy and distracted so no further change comes about.

We now move to the Fourth House.

FOURTH HOUSE

Home

Melanie has the *Teacher* at the Symbolic or Conscious level. More wonderful news as this says that she is ready to learn this old lesson and begin to walk her walk, and talk her talk.

This says that she's getting ready to finish off old ways of doing things and to let go of the roles that she's learned from her parents or culture. She is now ready to be true to herself and follow her own pathway.

It means she can now trust in the support she's getting from her own inner wisdom and trust in her heart's guidance, but she keeps herself from this guidance by doing judgment and criticism. Melanie's *"Child"* wants her to stay safe by playing old roles, but this doesn't need to be the way any longer.

So far, everything we've looked at is at the Individuation or Symbolic level, so this is all nuisance value stuff, it's not life threatening or major. If it was Tribal, it would be much more difficult to shift.

Now let's explore the Tenth House.

TENTH HOUSE

Highest Potential

Melanie has the *Saboteur* at the Individuation or Sub Conscious level. What this is saying is that to move to her highest potential or her destiny, she has to stop sabotaging herself with employing old values and old thinking.

But only Melanie can do this work, as no one can give you a pill and say, "All fixed, your mindset is now changed." This is where discipline comes in, as well as commitment, focus and self-love.

Not everyone has this level of commitment. A lot of people talk about it, but very few live it. The *Child* within Melanie is still deciding whether to stop sabotaging herself, by staying with the Child's map of the world, or move to a higher perspective and let her heart guide her.

Sometimes, to take our power back from the fearful *Child*, we just have to put our big girl or big boy pants on and grow up.

Let's move to the Fifth House.

FIFTH HOUSE

Love and Creativity

Traditionally known as the House of Children, this house is about love, creativity, passion and joy, and obviously any children you have or influence.

Melanie has *Myth* at the Tribal or Unconscious level. This is the first stumbling block we encounter. I believe it's the Tribal or Unconscious levels that are the true gifts in the chart, as these are the archetypes that say, "pay attention."

The Symbolics say, "well done, you've got a handle on this," but the Tribals are the red flags asking you to wake up.

So the Fifth house is saying that Melanie is losing her power to the past, because of the *Myth*, believing that whatever she is doing will keep her safe somehow. But it's not true!

In my map of the world, if **any** Archetype is sitting at Tribal or the Unconscious level in the Fifth house, it's saying you're doing way too much thinking, and you're not having enough fun, creativity, play, laughter or relaxation to bring about more balance in your life. You're not exploring your passions either.

So the Fifth house is saying two things to Melanie – "Stop thinking so much and start using your right brain more, and really examine what it is that you're stuck in the past about?" The clue is in the Eleventh House and the Ninth House.

Now we move to the Eleventh House.

ELEVENTH HOUSE

Relationship to the World

Melanie has *Caretaker* at the Tribal level. This is a danger sign because this House is about your future potential, your hopes, dreams and wishes. It represents the bigger picture and your relationship to the world.

This is saying that Melanie is stuck in believing she has to stay safe by looking after others and always taking care of others. She believes that if she doesn't, her world will come crashing down. It's time to ask Melanie how and where she learned this role?

The Fifth/Eleventh house combination in Melanie's chart is a major warning sign as she has a Tribal opposite another Tribal. She also has this combination in the Sixth/Twelfth houses as well. We need to pay attention to this as it's buried deep within and can be a pitfall. It's time to bring this to the surface so that Melanie can choose which way she wants to live her life.

Let's go to the Sixth house.

SIXTH HOUSE

Work and Health

If there's a major warning on the chart, then this is it. Why? Because anything at the Tribal level in the 6th house says that if you don't listen to the whispers, you may have to hear a shout!

Melanie has *Prostitute* at the Tribal level. The *Prostitute* asks, "How are you selling yourself short and how are you putting yourself out of your integrity?"

Melanie is doing this by believing that she has to keep busy, *caretaking* everyone else, and this belief keeps her stuck in the past (Myth). She stops herself from opening up to her creativity, her joy and passion.

She is also thinking way too much and these beliefs are all selling her short and may mean a wake up call via illness or something happening at work. It's only a potential, but still possible.

Yet there is a core part of her that wants to do things differently, such as the *Teacher*, the *Prince/Princess* and the *Philosopher* Archetypes. But which part will she listen to?

That's the big question and only Melanie can answer that for herself.

Please note: Never make a blanket statement to someone that they're going to get ill, if you're doing a chart reading for another. No matter what the chart is saying, it's potential only and nothing is written in concrete.

Let's now move to the Twelfth House.

TWELFTH HOUSE

Collective Soul, Hidden, the Unconscious

Melanie has the *Perfectionist* sitting at the *Tribal* or Unconscious level in this house. For many lifetimes, Melanie has had the viewpoint that as long as she's perfect in this world, then she'll stay safe.

Of course this belief is what is victimising her (First House). She brought this belief in with her, as it's very old indeed. Anything in the Twelfth house at Tribal usually means it's very old.

It's a dangerous Archetype at the Tribal level as it can mean illness in some form or another to help you wake up from this illusion, particularly being opposite the Sixth House. Debilitating issues like migraines, stress based symptoms around the skin, gut or reproductive organs, to name a few, are possible. It's opposite the Prostitute (one of the main four), also at Tribal, so this combination also says, "pay attention!"

SUMMARY

The chart is revealing to Melanie that her old beliefs say she must take care of others and be what they want her to be. But is this really true? Her inner critic judges either herself or others and is not helpful.

She can ignore this information, but it may be at her own peril. The sixth house is saying it's time to stop doing the same old behaviors. These beliefs are lifetimes old. They're based on martyrdom and sacrifice. It would be helpful to replace them with creativity, better boundaries, more self worth and self-love.

Melanie is totally supported now by her own Higher Self as well as her own innate wisdom and intuition, but she has to remember to tap into these parts of herself.

Many times after doing a chart reading, the client is sitting there in tears. This is because the Chart has struck a deep chord within. I truly don't believe I'm telling the client something they don't already know, it just depends how honest they are with themselves.

I would then discuss with the client if they would like to make some changes in their life. We discuss how they may potentially go about making this happen. I ask what sort of support they need to make all this possible? I have mentioned some ways of doing this in Chapter Ten.

Given that I've only ever had one person in the approximately twenty thousand chart readings disagree vehemently with what the chart was saying, then I have to conclude that the charts don't lie.

I trust you too will find this out for yourself. Don't take my word for it. Play and explore and see what unfolds. It's an exciting adventure to be sure.

10

PRACTICAL TOOLS

HOW TO MAKE CHANGE

It's one thing to see what the chart is saying, but it's quite another to know how to move it or change it somehow.

What do *you* do when you're feeling out of control, stuck, lethargic, or anxious for example? There is no blanket statement to fix every situation, as on one level, every situation is unique. At another level, it's all a game being played by psychological mind.

What we tend to do is get caught up in overthinking everything, playing the drama out over and over again: "I should have done that." "I could have said this!" Perhaps your mind says, "If only they didn't react that way everything would be all right." "Maybe I should have turned left instead of right." It's like being caught on a mouse's wheel that just goes round and round, going over old territory ad infinitum.

The good news is that there are indeed many helpful hints, but it's remembering to employ them and become good at them.

It starts with the acceptance of "what is" - of where your life is right now. Your past is gone, it's happened and now you have to deal with the present moment. Your decisions from the past have impacted on you and led you to this very moment. It's called taking full responsibility for what's been created in your life, even though you may not have planned any of it at the conscious level.

LETTING GO OF MONKEY MIND

Now the tricky bit happens. If you can remember to just feel the pain of whatever is arising, whatever is pressing your buttons, **and not use your thoughts** to go over and over old territory, then usually the distressing feeling will leave after a while.

"What," you say. "How can that happen when my mind is always there? It's impossible not to think?"

The thing that keeps us on the mouse's wheel is identifying with our mind. We think our mind is what we are, when in fact our mind is just a tool. We simply haven't yet been taught how to use it wisely. Most of us are a slave to our minds, whereas, in my opinion, we need to learn how to master the mind. Another way to say this is that mind has become our guru, whereas the true master is our heart and mind needs to be the student.

Why don't you try this next time a little drama pops up in your life. Not a big drama, just a little one to start off with. Let's say someone is rude to you at a restaurant, or in the supermarket. Your immediate reaction is to feel offended. You may want to shrink away or confront this person and start telling them off.

One of the things you can do is to locate the feeling in your body. It may resemble anger, shame, indignation, rage, or any of the so-called negative feelings that we all have. Perhaps this feeling is sitting in your gut? Maybe it's in your shoulders, your heart or jaw? It could be anywhere in fact.

Locate this feeling and just sit with it **but do not attach thinking to the feeling**. No mind, no judgment, no retort - just sit with the feeling. There are no new feelings by the way, just old ones waiting to come up and be healed.

If you can sit with the feeling and just allow it to be there, without allowing your mind to intervene, then very soon the feeling will go away. It's the attachment of thought through judgment or projection that does the damage and keeps you in pain and suffering.

I totally understand that it's not always possible to just allow the feeling to be there, without thinking. You may be driving, or in an emergency situation of some sort, but where possible and in the right circumstances, try this out and see what unfolds.

You may have to do this many times a day, but the more you can simply feel, let go of thinking, then the quicker the negativity or toxicity can move on. I know this seems simplistic, but don't dismiss it until you've tried it.

The feeling generated by the incident will be an old feeling, still stuck in the body, from some other time and place where you did not get the opportunity to feel into it. Instead you suppressed it and buried it within.

By feeling into it, without your mind attached, you have an opportunity to let go of a chemical reaction, induced by emotions that cause toxicity in the body. The person in the supermarket or restaurant is simply being a catalyst in your life to allow these old feelings to surface and move on.

But you have to catch them and be aware that this is what's happening. I'm not talking about denial here. I'm talking about allowing the feelings to simply BE, without sticking on a label of good or bad, right or wrong. Just allowing and Being.

We do need our thinking mind, especially practical mind or creative mind, as it helps you to drive a car or build things, plan a holiday or write a Thesis.

But the damage is done by false mind. That part of you that wants you to think, think and then think again ad infinitum. Doing all this thinking stops you from finding the peace within that will start the healing process.

BEING PRESENT

Another thing to try is to simply be **Present** in the moment. Even though anger or frustration, perhaps even rage is erupting within you, allow it to be there and come back to the body and simply notice your senses. Come away from your mind and the thought forms (which is where all the anger emanates from), and just feel the senses.

Notice your breathing or feel the pulses in your body. Be aware of people around you, notice how they're standing or sitting, just be aware, but without judgement. This is a skill that takes time to develop. It asks you to be aware of where your mind is. Now go back to the breath. By doing this, you call your energy back into the Present moment.

You cannot **truly** be in the Present moment, completely aware of the present while **thinking** at the same time. It's impossible.

Afterwards, you may get a sense of what thinking was going on that produced the stress and unhappiness.

In most situations, the present moment is not causing your unhappiness, it's the thinking from the past or projecting into the future, that generates the feeling behind it.

There are many wonderful modalities out there that can help you shift old thinking, heal old wounds and toxic programming so that you can lead a more fulfilling and happier life.

SUGGESTIONS

The sort of help you receive does depend on where you live geographically on the planet. It may also depend on what your financial resources are. You may also want to feel into the possibility of going mainstream like psychologists or psychiatrists or perhaps you'd prefer more alternative therapies such as those listed below.

I have used all the therapies mentioned, either as a practitioner of it or as a client. I can recommend them all, but at the end of the day, it's an individual choice.

- **Emotional Freedom Technique** or EFT for short. This is a "tapping" technique that works on the meridian circuits in the body, or energy centres. According to Wikipedia: **Emotional Freedom Techniques (EFT)** is a form of counseling intervention that draws on various theories of alternative medicine including acupuncture, neuro-

linguistic programming, energy medicine,
and Thought Field Therapy (TFT). There are
practitioners all over the world because of its
popularity, so go to the Internet to find out who feels
right for you to work with, if this appeals to you.

- **Regression Therapy**. This usually involves
hypnosis and takes you back to the seat of trauma to
resolve it. Some people find this very effective, but it
can depend on the practitioner and your willingness
to let go.

- **Kinesiology**. This may include muscle testing,
touch for health, kinergetics and applied physiology.
It helps to reduce emotional trauma and release
blockages around a variety of issues, as well as
working on physical pain.

- **Cutting the Ties that Bind** based on the work of
Phyllis Krystal. You may buy her books and guide
yourself through these techniques or find a qualified
practitioner. This work bypasses the conscious mind
and works at a deeper, sub conscious level. It has been
highly effective for many and I've been using it for
over 20 years.

- **Breath Work**, often used in conjunction with
hypnosis, but also stands alone. It releases stress from
the body and resolves trauma. Find a good
practitioner who is skilful and experienced in this
modality.

- **Meditation**. There are many different forms of
meditation. It is scientifically proven to reduce stress
and physical ailments. It's worth trying many
different forms to see which one appeals to you, but
it is highly effective and always recommended.

Sound healing meditations come into this category as well.

- **Reiki/Seichim**. I have been a Reiki/Seichim Master since 1993. All variations to Reiki are worth learning as it teaches you about energy and how to use it on yourself or on others, via Absentee Healings.
- **Matrix Energetics**. The originator of this modality is Richard Bartlett. His classes are found on the Internet. Richard teaches you how to use different energy techniques to bring about healing and move beyond limited thinking.
- **Sacred Ceremony**. I know several teachers who do this work where I am based. You use the healing properties of Nature to let go of things that no longer serve you; some use different plant medicines or the energies of the full or new moons.
- **Trauma release**. There are many different ways to release trauma from the body. One popular one is called TRE – tension, stress and trauma release work. There are practitioners of this all over the world.

USING YOUR RIGHT BRAIN

If you're used to thinking all the time, don't stop to play or have fun, then it's time to start your creative process going so that you can open up to your right brain, your hidden treasure chest within.

It may be that you need to open up to learning to draw, paint or do mandalas. Maybe it's working with clay or ceramics that gives you a buzz.

There's a helpful book called *The Artist's Way,* by Julia

Cameron – she takes you step by step into your right brain. In my experience, this book only works well when you do all of it, not just choose bits and pieces.

Right now, there's a plethora of coloring and drawing books out there in the market place, so there does not need to be a huge expense involved in opening up to your right brain and finding out more of who you really are.

There is another book I can highly recommend: *101 Strategies for True Health and Empowerment,* by Robyn Wood. In this book are many different suggestions and modalities that may help with regard to any issue that you're facing or dealing with. Robyn's website is: www.robynmwood.com/book/

SPIRITUAL STUDY

You may prefer to study with a group to expand your awareness about your true nature. *A Course in Miracles* comes to mind. ACIM groups meet all around the world.

Eckhart Tolle, a modern spiritual teacher now offers many Courses in spiritual development, via the Internet. So do many other teachers.

Some people prefer to work with the ancient spiritual, esoteric teachings, while others prefer to find a Master teacher on the planet and study with them or experience their form of spirituality. It's almost overwhelming what comes up when you do a search on the Internet.

Whatever it is that you undertake, always but always trust your inner knowing and heart to give you feedback about the efficacy and integrity of the person you choose to learn from or with.

The Internet is a wonderful resource for exploring who is in your local area that can help you. There are many websites that have group platforms where you can join to receive support and guidance. They may be half away around the world but they can still be perfect for your growth.

There are a plethora of skills out there but not all of them will suit you, so it's a matter of trusting that your Higher Self will guide you to the right modality, at the relevant time. With the Internet so freely available to nearly all of us, you can find so many different ways of delving into your own true nature, but discernment must be exercised here, as there are a lot of charlatans ready to take advantage of your enthusiastic naivety.

Please remember to be gentle on yourself, there's no need to rush or believe that it has to happen immediately or even to get it all done yesterday. You've taken quite a while to get to this place and it may take a bit longer to remember who you really are. It's all unfolding; just trust in the process and your inner guidance.

At the end of the day, the whole point to this exercise is to learn to allow and trust your feelings as opposed to listening to your thinking mind all the time. We need to learn to feel and trust so we can live more easily in our hearts.

This is a critical step to empowerment, to understanding that you're a Conscious Being who has choice in how you respond to all situations. This is moving from the Tribal level to the Individuation level.

Beyond this point, at the Symbolic or Conscious level you begin to understand that even your emotions/feelings, along with your thoughts, are not necessarily the real you either. Your feelings and thoughts are the result of your programming and come from your beliefs inherited from your Tribe or Culture.

Once you learn how to drop out of thinking mind, into the deep peace within, then a whole new world awaits you where you will co-create with your Higher Self or Spirit.

You can learn how to live in freedom beyond the ideologies that you have been taught and free yourself from much of the pain and suffering that goes with mind and the old programs.

Thank you for taking the time to read this book. I hope you have gained something from it or even better, cast your own chart.

I have had the privilege of having done a plethora of Archetype Chart Readings and the same amount of healings on people. This has been a wonderful journey into self-discovery. The mirror has been alive and well as looking into others has meant looking into myself. I have learned to trust in Spirit completely. I know this is my true nature as it is yours as well.

My dream has been to share this wonderful tool with as many people who want to learn it. I wish you well on your journey. It is my sincere desire that you know that you are always loved and supported, even when it does not feel like it.

It's time to change how we live on this magnificent planet and it starts with each one of us. Our internal chaos mirrors the outer chaos in the world, so the true healing journey starts with us.

As Gandhi says, "Be the change you wish to see in the world."

I like to say, "Be the LOVE you wish to see in the world."

Blessings to each and every one of you.

11

ASTROLOGICAL WHEEL EXPLANATION

We use the astrological wheel as a foundation referring only to the houses in the zodiac.

There are so many good books out there that explain about the Houses in Astrology so you may care to expand your knowledge apart from what I'm sharing with you in this book.

Here is a brief explanation of the houses as I see it, looking through the lens of the Archetypes. You may also view this in video format by going to my website:

www.archetypechartreadings.com.

ASTROLOGICAL HOUSES

First House

This house is also known as the Ascendant or Rising Sign, in astrological terms. It is the establishment of your personal identity or the face you show the world. It's not necessarily the real YOU, but the mask you wear. This house covers your personal affairs, physical appearance and physical make up. It's how the world sees you and the social persona you give out. It also represents new beginnings.

Second House

Your values sit here. The traditional name is The House of Money. This is where your self-esteem, self worth and self respect sit. It represents what you value most. It is the "inner" you that only your closest friends may know.

Suggestion: Archetypally, it's a challenge here if you have anything at the Tribal or Unconscious level as it usually means there is unfinished business going on from your childhood. You may be holding onto beliefs that no longer serve you such as "I'm not good enough." Or perhaps you need other people's approval before you can make a decision?

Third House

This house represents your Will and how you use it. Traditionally known as The House of Communication, it includes our relationship to the environment (global and local). This is the way you think and how you communicate to others. It's also how others hear you, as well as how you talk to your Higher Self or listen to your Inner Critic. It is also the house of siblings and short journeys. Education sits here as well.

Suggestion: If anything is Tribal here, it often means the person does not take the necessary time out to listen to their heart or their inner wisdom, but only focuses on what the rational mind is saying.

Fourth House

Traditionally known as The House of Home, it represents how you use your personal power. Does the need to manipulate or control come from your mind or your heart? This represents your childhood home, or it can mean your current home, perhaps the planet as home as well as your body as home. Real estate sits here.

It is also represents your relationship to your own mother. It is your private self and possibly more the ***real you*** than the first house. It feels to me like your soul essence sits here as well.

Suggestion: Archetypally, if anything is Tribal here, it may suggest that there is deep unfinished business to complete from your childhood, particularly with your mother. It depends on which Archetype shows up.

Fifth House

This house explores how you use your creativity and sexuality, how you give love and receive love. Traditionally known as The House of Children, it refers to biological children as well as adopted or inherited children. This house can also refer to gambling, hobbies and recreation. This is the house for love affairs, romance, joy and passion.

Suggestion: If anything is Tribal here, it often means the person does too much thinking and does not take enough time to play, have fun, relax and just chill out. It can also mean that they do not express themselves creatively and have shut down the right side of their brain.

. . .

Sixth House

This is the house of work and health. It also includes your relationship to service, pets, habits, duty and unequal relationships. It is the least free house in the whole Chart.

Suggestion: Anything Tribal or Unconscious sitting here is a big warning sign as it often means that the person is not listening to the whispers and may need to receive a shout to wake up. It's a hard way to learn life's lessons, via illness or losing a job. However, everything is only a potential.

Seventh House

The House of Partnerships, though the traditional name is The House of Marriage. It represents our significant one on one relationships, to our partner, friends, colleagues, workmates, peer group, family, as well as those who challenge you or assist you.

Co-dependency can show up in this house, or it may show how much you allow others to dominate you, depending on the Archetype. Of course, the ultimate one on one relationship is to the Self and through the Self to the Higher Self.

Suggestion: If something is Tribal here, it may mean the person is having a hard time trusting in their Higher Self or listening to their intuition.

Eighth House

The House of Death, Sex and shared resources, but also the house of transformation. This house can indicate inheritances and insurance benefits. It shows important changes in life and your reaction to them. It also deals with sexual expression and regeneration.

Suggestion: Archetypally speaking, I feel this House has a lot to do with your life's lesson, what you've come here to transcend or transform.

Ninth House

This rules your philosophical and religious outlook on life. It is about our search for meaning. It is also about higher education and how you pursue your vocation in life to broaden your outlook. Metaphysics and the Higher Mind sit here. It is also the house for publishing. This house may represent your capacity to communicate with your Higher Self.

Tenth House

This house rules your career and conscious ambition, destiny and highest potential. Traditionally known as The House of Career. It is our public image and reputation. Your relationship to authority figures can sit here as it also represents your relationship to your father.

Suggestion: If anything is Tribal here, it may mean unfinished business from childhood, especially with the father.

Eleventh House

The house of hopes, dreams and wishes. Traditionally known as The House of Friends, it represents our social interactions and ideals. It can represent your relationship to the world. I often see this house as representing the future; your visions and dreams sit here as well as global awareness.

Suggestion: If a Tribal Archetype sits here, it's a warning about potentially sabotaging yourself from fulfilling your highest possible dreams.

Twelfth House

This house represents the hidden or the unconscious and the collective soul, but it's traditionally known as The House of Troubles. It may represent secrets we keep hidden from ourselves. It is also the house of karma and transcendence so can show you what you've been unable to finish in other lifetimes and how you've held yourself back. It can also hold our hidden strengths, depending on what Archetype shows up.

Suggestion: If a Tribal Archetype shows up, it indicates that whatever it is that you're trying to achieve in this lifetime is very, very old.

12

THE ARCHETYPES AND THEIR MEANINGS

Here is a list of all of the Archetypes I use, with their meanings at the Unconscious and Conscious Levels of Awareness.

The first four archetypes (Child, Victim, Prostitute, and Saboteur) are included in every reading.

CHILD

Tribal: Fear and old programming immobilizes the Child. It tenaciously holds onto old beliefs because it would rather have the familiar than the unknown, as the latter is terrifying. There are many variations to the Child, such as the Spoilt Child, the Wounded Child or something called the Puer Aeternus, which is the "Peter Pan" syndrome of the child who never wants to grow up. Michael Jackson was the classic of this Archetype. Then there's the Entitled Child which has more prominence now due to the Millennials. They expect instant gratification.

The Child at the Unconscious level is emotionally unavailable and needs to get its own way all the time. It also has trouble growing up and hearing a deeper truth. When things don't go the way the Child wants, it will simply throw a temper tantrum. But behind this behaviour are many clues with regard to what the Child is really feeling. You can be playing out this Archetype, at this level, even if you're in your eighties.

> *Ask Yourself: Does your inner Child look like this? What's the payoff to staying in your Child at this level? How are you avoiding being responsible? What are my biggest fears and are they even valid?*

Symbolic: The Child only wants to live in their truth, he or she wants to get on with life and achieve their highest potential. The Child is not prepared to let anything or anyone get in the way anymore, but they achieve their goals with maturity and kindness. They are emotionally available to others, they respond to situations instead of reacting.

VICTIM

Tribal: The Victim is powerless and believes everyone or everything is conspiring against him or her. There is no responsibility taken for what has unfolded in life. The Victim at this level needs to blame everyone else for what's happening. They get to feel hopeless and helpless and often believe that someone else has to do it for them to bring about change. At this point in the earth's journey, there is a strong Victim consciousness everywhere on the planet. In other words, it's everyone else's fault and nothing to do with you at all.

> *Ask Yourself: We can play the Victim in some areas of our lives, but not in others. Where does it play out most in your*

life? Whom or what do you need to blame for what's happened in your life? How hard is it for you to take responsibility for your life?

Symbolic: You take your power back from this belief and know you're creating your own reality. You understand that your thoughts are energy in motion, so you take responsibility for what you're thinking, which in turn empowers you to make change and move on with your life. You understand that everything is connected, so what you feel, think and do is all part of the Whole and has a ripple effect on everything in your life.

PROSTITUTE

Tribal: You're selling yourself short or putting yourself out of your integrity, often by playing old roles that no longer serve you. There is a need to win approval, or be valued, liked or loved. You are not true to yourself at all. In fact, you may not even know what your real truth looks like as you're so used to giving your power away to others. This can have dangerous consequences down the track resulting in illness.

Ask Yourself: How do you sell yourself short? How are you NOT living in your integrity by still playing old roles? What's the payoff to stay stuck? What's the lure that keeps you there?

Symbolic: You refuse to sell yourself short for anyone or anything. You stand up for yourself, or walk away when you know the situation is untenable. You will not be put down by anyone as your inner strength is established and you know your own values. You march to the beat of your own drum, instead of what society tells you. You are able to see what you're doing and change the situation without shame or regret, as you see everything as a learning curve and there for your highest good. You accept "what is."

SABOTEUR

Tribal: Self-sabotage can be done in many ways, such as not having enough money, or by being ill with health issues, perhaps denying your emotions and not honoring them. You may bring someone into your life that is so needy, you never get to live your own passion or desires, so you'll constantly sabotage yourself to keep others safe. Your belief systems can sabotage you as you believe you're not enough in some way. There are countless ways in which we do this. This person may always be in the mind, only believing in the rational or scientific model and therefore does not listen to inner wisdom.

> *Ask Yourself: What does sabotage look like for you? Does this play out regularly in your life? If so, what fears keeps you playing this old role? Are they even valid? What will it take for you to do things differently?*

Symbolic: You wake up to the game and refuse to play it any more. You will not let anyone sabotage your highest potential, including your own monkey mind, as you see it for the old, inherited programming it really is. You do what it takes to become strong and healthy or move on from old relationships that no longer serve you. Your own self worth and self love become a high priority now, in equality with the caring and nurturing of those that you love.

ACTOR

Tribal: At this level, the Actor only feels safe when playing roles given by others. These roles may come from the parents, or other authority figures or quite literally, the Director of the stage play. The Actor needs the accolades from the audience or others, to validate how good they are. They must have the applause to feel like they're worthwhile.

They usually have no idea who they are, when off-stage, as there is no inner reference point around self worth. This means they have no deep understanding of themselves and can be easily led astray by flattery and hype.

> *Ask Yourself: What roles are you playing to please others? What's the payoff to playing these old roles?*

Symbolic: At this level, the Actor knows who they are on and off stage. If they play a role they can easily leave it behind once they leave the "stage." Their self worth is not tied up in the approval. This Actor can inspire, create, and serve well, without hidden agendas.

ADVOCATE

Tribal: The Advocate rushes into help others, advocating on their behalf, as it makes them feel good to do this. This Archetype is akin to the Rescuer, Helper and Caretaker. They often work in the public arena, be it social work or the court system.

They like others to see them as a great person. At this Tribal or Unconscious level, it means the Advocate has to play this role at the physical level and can often exhaust themselves in the process.

> *Ask Yourself:* Are you advocating too much on behalf of others to the detriment of yourself? Why do you do this to yourself?

Symbolic: At this level, they may still help others, but they equally help themselves. The Advocate has no need to be approved of, by others, as there is no self-aggrandizement. They do the job well and can then walk away, trusting in the process.

ALCHEMIST

Tribal: The Alchemist is about transformational energy. Metaphorically, this person is capable of turning "lead into gold" or "water into wine," using a combination of chemistry, magic and philosophy. But they can misuse their power to benefit only themselves in a material manner.

The other side of the coin is that they're capable of manifesting things but won't because they're frightened of their own power.

Still another aspect to this Archetype is that they create alchemy for others, but forget to do it for themselves because of lack of self worth issues.

> *Ask Yourself:* How do you create Alchemy in your own life, or do you just do it for others? Do you use your power well, for the good of the whole, or do you use it to manipulate?

Symbolic: The Alchemist's work is spiritually based, and is all about transformational energy, working for the higher good.

They are tuned in at the Higher Self level and follow their inner guidance that serves all.

Alchemy can mean someone comes to visit you; they arrive feeling awful, they have a cup of tea with you and an hour later, they feel great. Or it could be the person who has recovered from cancer as they have transformed their life completely. It's all Alchemy!

ANIMAL

Tribal: This person can literally prefer the Animal Kingdom to the Human Realm. They feel safer with animals, particularly dogs and horses, which are so very loyal and give out unconditional love.

This Archetype, at this level, can mean that they do not trust their human companions as usually they've been betrayed somewhere along the line, by a lover, a parent, a good friend, work scenarios or even one's own health.

> *Ask Yourself: The issue is feeling abandoned or betrayed, so the question to ask is who or what are you NOT trusting? Is it another or yourself? Why?*

Symbolic: This person has learned the lessons behind the betrayal and can trust humans as much as animals. They no longer have to hide behind animals to receive the love they want as they can be at peace with either animals or humans. They have learned to TRUST and have taken responsibility for all that has unfolded in their life.

ARTIST

Tribal: Includes all levels of creativity. At the Tribal level, the Artist often has low self-esteem or else they deny their abilities because of others putting them down at some point, be it teachers or parents and so forth.

It can also mean that it's time to create, literally, in the physical world, be it drawing, painting, ceramics or writing. But the fear that it won't be good enough gets in the way. The Artist may also create for others, but not for themselves.

At this level, the Artist may be asking you to write a whole new script for yourself, or paint a whole new canvas as to how you wish your life to be.

> *Ask Yourself: How safe are you to express your creativity and live it? What's stopping you? Is it time to create a new life for yourself?*

Symbolic: At this level, they're a direct channel for Divine Will, be it in the written, spoken or artistic realm. They let go and let God and allow it all to come through them. They may not even have to bring artistic skills into form as they happen on other levels, in other realms. There's no fear in expressing the real self and sharing their gifts with the world.

BLANK CARD

Tribal: You can create any new archetype with this card. It's about the unknowable, the hidden or new beginnings, in fact anything you wish to create that takes you on a new pathway.

The future is yours if you'll have the courage to follow your intuition.

This card is saying that you can now paint any picture you want or write any story for yourself, particularly in the physical reality. At this level however, not knowing the future plan is too scary, as you do not feel safe or in control. There's no trust in your ability to create this new story.

> *Ask Yourself: What do you yearn to create but are too frightened to step into? What stops you from trusting in yourself to start a new life in some way?*

Symbolic: At this level, they are totally able to trust in the Divine and do not need to know how it will all play out, as they're able to drop into their heart's guidance. They live in the moment, let life unfold and simply deal with whatever is arising because of the connection to Spirit.

CARETAKER

Tribal: This person has to take care of others, or else they have no true meaning in life. This belief can lead to Chronic Fatigue, among many other illnesses.

There's a certain level of arrogance that goes with this archetype, as they don't believe that people can look after themselves, **so they must do it for them.** Parents can easily play this role. They often ignore their own needs and this archetype can easily link in with the Martyr. The belief is, "I'm not valid unless I'm taking care of others." Self-care usually doesn't happen at this level.

Ask Yourself: How are you not taking care of yourself, on all levels, physically, mentally, emotionally, spiritually and financially? What keeps you doing this, even when you're exhausted?

Symbolic: They can still look after others, but equally know how to look after themselves. They have the wisdom to know when to step back and allow others to take on board their own responsibility for their life choices, attitudes and perceptions. They have clear boundaries and can say NO when necessary.

CATALYST

Tribal: This Archetype is great at being the catalyst for everyone's growth, but not their own. They may say, "Why don't you read this book, see this healer or do that course?" They can live vicariously through others as well, exhausting themselves, as the catalyst role takes over their life.

Ask Yourself: Are you catalyzing everyone else's opportunities except your own? If so, why, what's the payoff?

Symbolic: At this level, the Catalyst has the balance and wisdom to know when to do something for others and when to step back. The busyness syndrome is seen as a smoke screen that has been created to stop helping themselves and they can therefore bring the balance back into their own life.

CELIBATE

Tribal: In this column, the Celibate is frightened of sexual expression and can lead to perverted behavior or complete shutdown of the pelvic/genital area. They avoid intimacy at all costs and will do anything to put up brick walls. It could mean they're always working hard, have lots of illness, no self-esteem, shyness, a gruff exterior and so on.

Usually their role models for intimacy are abysmal and sexual abuse <u>may</u> have happened in their childhood. They may have been hurt to the core in a romantic relationship and swear to never venture into those dark waters again. They do not know how to trust or let intimacy in. It has to start with the Self however.

> <u>Ask Yourself</u>: What frightens you the most about true intimacy? Are you capable of being vulnerable and feeling exposed with another person? Why do you need to protect yourself? Are you caring for yourself, truly understanding what your needs are and then meeting them?

Symbolic: Now the Celibate transmutes sexual energy into alternative forms of expression, often to higher levels, perhaps creatively and artistically. They can take or leave relationships, but there is no fear present with regard to being in an intimate relationship. Most importantly, they have an intimate relationship with their higher self; they know themselves, their passions, and their desires and live in their integrity.

CLOWN/FOOL

Tribal: This person has little common sense or discernment, and often acts unwisely. They may act the clown to win approval or avoid difficulties such as confrontation. They rarely honor themselves and may avoid speaking their truth. They can use the mask of the Clown so that others won't see their real pain.

The Fool characteristic can be very naïve and often does not follow through on plans or do their homework around a particular situation. They cannot see that they are about to walk over the cliff edge because they're simply not paying attention.

> *Ask Yourself*: What mask are you hiding behind or what are you doing to avoid dealing with the truth? Are you present when you're doing something or do you have a tendency to **not** pay attention?

Symbolic: The clown/fool knows how to turn pain into laughter for the highest good. They are no-one's fool. They no longer need to wear a mask as they deal with issues as they arise. There can even be a mystical connection, as they stand naked before Source. The inner and outer match, as what you see is what you get. They follow through and take responsibility for all that is going on in their life.

CONFIDANTE

Tribal: This person is great at listening to everyone's story as it wins him or her approval. But they do not listen to their own inner guidance. They also usually don't feel "heard" by others. They often have unclear boundaries, perhaps by listening to other people's dramas even when they don't want to.

> *Ask Yourself*: Why are you always listening to others, even when you don't want to? What are you trying to avoid by not listening within? What's the fear around connecting to your Higher Self?

Symbolic: They can now easily hear others, but they also listen to their own inner guidance. They have clear boundaries in place and can say NO when they are too tired or simply don't care to hear the ongoing drama of other people's lives. At this level, the Confidante understands drama for what it really is, avoidance and distraction.

CONTROLLER

Tribal: The Controller at this level usually needs to be in control at all costs. It may also be that they allow others to control them for fear of being held responsible and perhaps making wrong choices.

Their biggest fear is being "out of control." So they may have to be in jobs that gives them "authority" and may need to feel superior to others. It may be overt control or covert. It is exhausting always having to be in control.

> *Ask Yourself: Why do you need to be in control all the time? What fears are behind this? Did you have a role model for this behavior?*

Symbolic: At this level, the Controller knows when to step up to the plate and take control, but equally knows when to step back and allow others to take the lead. They can be surrendered in chaos, knowing everything will pass and there are lessons in the chaos. They understand they have called it in for their growth, they may not like it, but accept it.

COWARD

Tribal: This person becomes immobilized by fear at this level. They need a gilt edged guarantee to take a "risk." They often give their power away to many things; usually fear based beliefs that tell then they're not safe. They believe that something will always go wrong or that they are not good enough. The Coward is often very cautious and careful, seeing the glass as half empty, rather than half full as fear calls the shots in most situations.

> *Ask Yourself: Who taught you how to do this? Where did you learn to be so fearful? Is it even true?*

Symbolic: At the Symbolic level, the Coward will not give their power away to fear or allow it to interfere with destiny. They feel the fear and do it anyway, see the fear as emanating from the mind and all its acquired beliefs. At this level, they live by their own inner truth and not the beliefs from their Tribe.

DETECTIVE/SLEUTH

Tribal: This Archetype is about finding out the facts. However, in the process of being the Detective, some may ride roughshod over others to get to this truth, in the name of righteousness. There may be little thought or concern for the other people involved in the story, as it's only about getting to the bottom line and who gets damaged along the way is irrelevant.

It may also be asking you to dig deeper to find out a bigger truth than the one you currently hold.

Ask Yourself: What do you need to explore or find out? How do you need to go about it so that you don't hurt anyone along the way?

Symbolic: At this level, there's a desire to find order in chaos, truth in deceit and structure in madness. But they also trust that they'll get exactly what they're meant to get. They do not harm others in the process. They look outside for answers as well as inside.

DISCIPLE

Tribal: The Disciple Archetype may give their power away to a teacher, Guru or cause. They may follow blindly, not use their own discernment or question things that do not feel right. They may also believe they can only get to "God" via an intermediary, such as the priest, rabbi or minister.

Of themselves, they are not "worthy," always the sinner and constantly striving to be good enough to get through the pearly gates of Heaven.

Ask Yourself: To what or whom are you blindly giving your power away? It may have religious overtones, but not always.

Symbolic: At this level, they see the teacher or Guru as a representation of the Divine Source and therefore, of themselves. They understand that Guru means "dispeller of darkness" and can show the illusions for what they are.

They are free to question and find own truth, allow their own heart to guide them and lead them to freedom. They trust implicitly in their connection to Source and see everything arising in the Divine Condition.

DISCIPLINARIAN

Tribal: At this level, one of two things happen – either no discipline at all, so in their physical world, they don't care what they eat, drink or if exercise never crosses their pathway.

The other aspect is to be over disciplined (from the fear of their life falling apart if they're not). They may be totally anal about how things must be, often going to extraordinary lengths to have things be a certain way so that discipline is maintained at all times. This Archetype is an adjunct to the Controller.

> *Ask Yourself: Do you lack discipline to carry out your highest potential, be it in your physical, emotional mental or spiritual world? What fear controls you that you have to be so overly disciplined?*

Symbolic: At this level, this person has balance. It is understood that they must have discipline to achieve their spiritual/material goals, but without fear attached, as they're trusting their heart to guide them to their highest truth. This person knows how to take a day off, have fun, lighten up, but also knows how to knuckle down and have commitment and focus.

DRAMA QUEEN

Tribal: As a generalization, this Archetype is often found in teenage girls, homosexual males or even some cultures. It's a way of being noticed, but is exhausting and manipulative. Everything may be prefaced with, "Oh My God!"

There is no inner peace at this level, as everything needs to be intense and full on. It may be his or her own drama or someone else's, just so long as it's drama, so they can get involved and lose themselves in "the story." It is avoidance of inner truth at the highest level.

> *Ask Yourself: Are you the Drama Queen and if so, what's the hook? How does it serve you to be this, what's the payoff? Does this role lead to harmony within?*

Symbolic: At this level, the Drama Queen is grounded, fully here and not projecting into the future or buying into drama of any sort. They no longer need to act out to be noticed. They have an inner knowing and see the Tribal level for the immature behavior it really is. They no longer need to avoid their own deep, inner truth by latching onto other people's dramas. They can step back and become the Observer, allowing it all to unfold around them, but not buy into it.

ENTERTAINER

Tribal: The Entertainer Archetype has to entertain others to be noticed. They must have the applause, or the recognition and be told how good or funny they are. It's similar to the Actor. The desire to be acknowledged is very strong as it may come from a place of not being seen or heard in childhood. Similar to the Actor.

It may also mean that you are born to be the entertainer but fear holds you back. This may look like "I'm not good enough!"

> *Ask Yourself: Why do you need to be the center of attention?*

*What does this feed within you? Are you using your gifts to
their fullest expression?*

Symbolic: At this level, the Entertainer may entertain but no
longer needs the accolades. They just come from the heart and
fulfill their passion for their own highest good. They have no
hidden agendas or false modesty. Their motivation is joy.

EQUIVOCATOR

Tribal: This Archetype is often misunderstood – they cannot
make up their mind so will sit on the fence like the Procrastinator. It's a fine line between these two Archetypes.

However, with the Equivocator, it is often because of laziness
or fear of speaking the truth that the procrastination occurs.
They fear being rejected if they speak their truth. They may
lack the discipline to get up and make things happen, so opt for
laziness instead.

*Ask Yourself: What are you reluctant to say? Is laziness
taking over your life and if so, why? Whose approval do you
still need?*

Symbolic: At this level, the Equivocator feels the fear and
speaks the truth. They will also get off their backside to make
things happen. They see the excuse of laziness for what it is -
the fear of stepping into their highest potential. They can see
that the fear of speaking their truth comes from the need for
approval from others.

ESCAPIST

Tribal: The Escapist runs away from anything fear based and this may be literal or metaphorical. We can escape in many different ways. Perhaps literally by making geographical changes. It could be mentally by not being present with people. Perhaps through drugs, television, movies, sports, sex, the mind, drama, illness, busyness, to name a few.

> *Ask Yourself: What are you running away from, physically, mentally, emotionally, spiritually or financially? Why do you need to escape your present circumstances?*

Symbolic: At this level, the Escapist confronts issues and has no need to run away from anything or anyone. They are totally present, open and available, to others as well as to themselves.

EXPLORER

Tribal: The Archetype of the Explorer loves finding out about things, be it in the physical or the mental realms. However, it can be used as a means of escape by constantly exploring and never feeling safe enough to put down their roots. The Explorer may have a fear of being trapped.

It may also mean that it's time to explore new fields, new ways of thinking or being, particularly in the physical world because it's Tribal.

> *Ask Yourself: Are you exploring because of the love of something, or are you avoiding something or someone you don't want to confront? Is this an old pattern? Are you stuck*

*in your life and too frightened to explore outside of your
comfort zone?*

Symbolic: The Explorer may still explore, either in the physical world or even other realms. Paradoxically the exploration can happen without having to even get out of their lounge chair. It means they can tap into higher levels of awareness, as they understand they are much more than their five senses. They are not running away from anything.

They understand they are here to experience as many different realities as possible so often go where others will not, but without fear, just following their heart's guidance and direction.

EXTROVERT

Tribal: This Archetype is similar to the Entertainer, as they love being the life of the party, they like to be noticed, or be the center of attention. This attitude conveys the statement, "The party can start now as I've arrived!"

> *Ask Yourself: Why do you need to be noticed or the center of attention? What's the payoff to being out there all the time?*

Symbolic: At this level, the Extrovert can still be the life of the party, but doesn't have to be. If it happens, it's not contrived in any way; it's a spontaneous event. They can also let others get the glory or fame, as they're not attached to the outcome. They understand that only the ego needs to be competitive and noticed.

FACILITATOR

Tribal: This Archetype usually facilitates other people's growth, and is often the one to get the workshop up and running. It keeps them busy and distracted, but they will not do the same for themselves.

The Facilitator usually likes to be in charge. It is similar energy to the Catalyst. They may like to have things done in a certain way or else they feel it will not be good enough.

> *Ask Yourself: Are you facilitating your own growth, or just other peoples? Do you believe that unless you do something, then it won't be done well by others?*

Symbolic: At this level, they now have good boundaries and balance between themselves and others. They do not have to be in charge or up front. They can be if they wish, but they can easily meld into the background. They have no need to be in charge of how things turn out. They facilitate their own growth as well as help others.

FANTASY

Tribal: These people are not grounded, or as the saying goes "the lights are on and no-one is home!" They live in a "Disneyland" reality, either as a way of escaping, or else they live in a fantasy world that they wished was true.

They don't want to see reality, as it's too unpalatable, painful and toxic, according to their perspective. They've may been physically or sexually abused as a child, but don't assume this to be the case. They may simply be running a very old memory that says, "I don't like being in a body, or on the earth plane."

Ask Yourself: Why is it too painful to be fully present and in your body? When did this feeling start? Why do you find a fantasy better than what is currently in your life? What can you do to change this around?

Symbolic: The Fantasy Archetype at this level has taken their power back from fantasyland and deals with reality how it is. They own they have created their reality to learn different life lessons. They learn how to forgive, move on and live according to their own heart's truth. They are fully present, in the now. They can tap into other realms, but they are always present and aware, totally in the body. There is no such thing as "going home" as home is where the heart is.

FOOL'S LOVE

Tribal: This Archetype continuously falls "in love" with the "wrong person" – and often it turns out to be the same betrayal issue over and over again. They believe that only when they're truly loved will everything be all right. They put it onto someone else to love him or her, instead of learning about self-love.

There's an idealized version of love happening here, the Disneyland map of the world that says, "Prince Charming will come and rescue me." If they're male, "The perfect Princess is out there waiting for me."

This Archetype may also become a doormat to someone else believing this is how to win someone's love. They may also be totally shut down around love because of betrayal and turn to the Animal or Nature kingdoms instead.

Ask Yourself: How do you sabotage yourself in love-based relationships? Are you true to yourself or do you give your power away?Where does your role model for intimacy and love come from? Does it serve you to keep this version going?

Symbolic: At the Symbolic level, the Fool's Love Archetype has learned their lessons around love, for they understand that only when self-love is present will they then attract in a similar vibration.

They stop looking outside of themselves for love, fill their own cup up first and get on with life. Often, out of left field, the wisest choice for them shows up, especially when they have stopped looking for someone to complete them, as they know there's no such thing. They're already whole and complete.

FRIEND

Tribal: The Friend Archetype at this level has no boundaries. They have to please others, believing that this is how they will be liked, loved and approved of, so they put their own needs aside. Often, they do not know how to befriend themselves. Even when they're exhausted, they will still do what others want them to do, as self-love does not exist.

Ask Yourself: Do you befriend yourself as much as you befriend others? If not, why? Do the words, "must", "should" or "have to" apply here, believing if you don't help others, something awful will happen!

Symbolic: This is the only place to have the Friend Archetype, as now they have clear boundaries and will speak their truth from their heart. They no longer suffer from the fear of rejection. They do not fear loss anymore as self-love has kicked in. His or her own integrity is worth more than being nice to another or trying to please someone else.

GOD/GODDESS

Tribal: One of the 'duality' archetypes, meaning it represents the masculine/feminine connection. This Archetype, at the Tribal/Unconscious level knows about the spiritual world, but doesn't want to pursue it or own it.

If they were brought up in a fundamentalist or orthodox religion, then it may be too frightening to step outside of the box and explore their own inner guidance. They would rather the safety of the "tribe" and its culture. It is challenging to stand independently and be seen as separate to the "tribe." There's often a passing interest in the world outside of orthodox religion but it seems too scary to go there.

This Archetype is also asking about the mind/heart connection as at this level, it often says it's separate and the mind is still very dominant and rules and the heart does not come into its own true power..

> *Ask Yourself:* Do you follow your own spiritual pathway or do you succumb to what the tribe tells says you should do? Are your beliefs about God truly yours or have you inherited them?
>
> Have you genuinely explored this pathway of your own volition? Does your mind still dominate over my heart? Are

you paying attention to your left-brain and not including your right brain?

Symbolic: At this level, they see the illusion and control for what it is - a fear based manipulative concept that gives the power to very few. They see Divine Source Energy as encompassing all, as opposed to the separation that is given via religion.

At this level of understanding, the heart has the true wisdom and guidance. It also means that the balance between the masculine and feminine is now in place, or the left brain/right brain connection is in balance and harmony.

GOOD GIRL/GOOD BOY

Tribal: Another duality archetype, representing the masculine and feminine in another way.

Everyone plays this role to a certain extent because we usually hear these words a lot in our childhood. At this level, playing this role is done out of fear of repercussions. Needing to stay the Good Girl or Good Boy as the adult means that you're not being true to yourself and it is akin to the Chameleon or Mascot Archetype.

Another way to say this is that you'll be what everyone else wants you to be so that you'll stay safe and supposedly loved by all. But there's a cost as it usually means you'll be out of your integrity by not being true to yourself.

Ask Yourself: Why do you need to please other people? What is the payoff? Did you play this role a lot as a child? Are you ready to step up your own truth and be who you want to be?

Symbolic: At the Symbolic level, the Good Girl/Boy is now in their integrity, walking their walk and talking their talk. They have taken their power back from what others think of them. They now have clear boundaries and can speak their truth. It means they now march to the beat of their own drum.

As a duality Archetype, it is also means that the left side (feminine) and right side (masculine) of their body, are now being equally represented and honored.

HEALER

Tribal: This Archetype often has hidden agendas around healing, such as needing to be seen as the healer/rescuer/helper/guru. They like to "heal" others as it makes them feel good. At this level the Healer believes they're doing the healing. They can also become addicted to doing this for others and never doing it for themselves.

Many healers at this level often become sick as they ignore their own needs and play out the Martyr and do not listen to their own internal wisdom. It may also mean that it's time to truly look at the self and heal old, unfinished business from within.

> *Ask Yourself: Do you help others to the detriment of yourself? What's the carrot that keeps you doing this for others and not for yourself? Are you ignoring what needs to be healed from within?*

Symbolic: The healer at this level understands it is the Divine Flow that does the healing; they are just the vessel for it and as such, connected to Source. They are able to trust and let it all unfold without directing and controlling the process, which means having zero investment in the outcome. They also walk their walk by attending to their own healing when necessary.

HERMIT

Tribal: At this level, this Archetype may be reclusive and withdrawn, because of past hurt. They will do anything to avoid relationship, as they don't trust others and may use the animal kingdom to replace the human one. Animals, particularly dogs and horses show unconditional love, so they're much safer to be around than the human realm. The Hermit Archetype often has no idea how to let love in, let alone give it out.

It can also mean that it's time to take a sabbatical, to go away on your own for a while, drop out of society and go within. This needs to be done on the physical level to gain wisdom from within.

> *Ask Yourself: Do you need to spend time alone? Do you avoid relationships with others and if so, why? Why are you so uncomfortable when you're around people?*

Symbolic: The Hermit may choose isolation for a higher purpose but does not avoid relationship in any way. At the Symbolic level, the Hermit may have a deep relationship to Nature as well as the Animal Kingdom, but not from avoidance. Instead, it's from the perspective of seeing the connection with all things.

HERO/HEROINE

Tribal: This too is a duality Archetype. At this level, there's a need to be rewarded and acknowledged for their heroic effort. It may be that they sell their story to a newspaper so that they can get the recognition they crave.

It can also mean that it's time to step up to the plate, find their inner courage to take the next step in their life. This will usually involve some sort of change in their physical world as it's Tribal.

Like all the duality Archetypes, it also asks about the relationship between the mind and the heart.

> *Ask Yourself: What is your motivation for being the Hero? Is it for recognition, or the thrill of the danger and the release of the endorphins? Which is dominant, your mind or your heart? Are you ignoring your own needs to always serve others?*

Symbolic: The Hero/Heroine has no need to be acknowledged or noticed. Their heroic acts are performed because that is what is called for in the moment. It is a human heart felt response without any motivation behind it.

This Archetype, at this level, has the courage to step up to the plate when required, but can easily blend into the background when necessary. The love of their fellow man may be the catalyst that ignites the Hero/Heroine within.

Like other duality Archetypes, it is the courage to be true to the self at this level, the blending and harmonizing of the inner Divine Masculine with the Divine Feminine. They do what it takes to be in their integrity and honor themselves, out of self-love, not narcissistic beliefs.

JUDGE

Tribal: We all share this archetype, as it's almost impossible not to judge, we're steeped in it. It comes from the need to feel superior or inferior to others and may be spoken or unspoken.

This Archetype is dangerous at the Tribal level as it can lead to illness later on in life such as arthritis, which, metaphysically speaking is hot anger stored in the joints. All judgment separates us out from our heart's truth as judgment comes from the mind.

> *Ask Yourself: Where did you learn judgment? Why do you do it? Is it out of automaticity? Are you even conscious of what words come out of your mouth? What feelings arise within when you judge others, or feel judged by others?*

Symbolic: At this level, judgment changes to discernment. Now wisdom takes over because of spiritual maturity and is aligned with your heart's highest truth. At the Symbolic level, this Archetype does not need to judge others in order to feel good about the self because their self-respect and love is from within. There is no need to feel superior or inferior as it's seen for the manipulation it truly is.

KING/QUEEN

Tribal: At this level, the King/Queen Archetype may be perceived as a dictator, destructive and egocentric. They feel superior to others; they do not understand the symbiotic relationship between King/Queen and subject. The Monarchy must have subjects or else there is nothing to rule. It is a perfect example of separation.

It is another version of the Mother/Father Archetype, both being part of the duality Archetypes in the pack.

> *Ask Yourself*: *Do you feel superior to others? Do you get a sense that you're better than others, or are you disconnected from people around you and therefore not in touch with reality?*

Symbolic: The King/Queen rules with wisdom and discernment for the highest good of all, totally understanding the unity of all.

At a personal level, it means you take back your own Sovereignty, and choose to come from the heart, which is your deepest truth. The Divine Masculine and the Divine Feminine is totally congruent and comes from discernment and love. Potentially, you have moved into Wholeness and therefore live in your authenticity and integrity.

KNOWER

Tribal: Not a well known Archetype as I made this one up a long time ago because I saw so much of this in people's energy fields.

The Knower may believe they "know it all." They may say, "I know" a lot. It usually means they have the intelligence without the wisdom. At this level, they feel they need to prove what they know or share their knowledge to be noticed and valued. They can often be seen as a "smarty-pants."

It may also mean that they hide their "knowing" because they've been ridiculed for it in the past. They may have old memories operating that tell them it's dangerous to know about things that are outside the "norm." So fear or arrogance can be behind the Knower at this level.

> *Ask Yourself: What are you frightened of knowing about yourself? Do you trust your inner Being to know the truth? Do you dumb yourself down to keep yourself safe?*

Symbolic: From the symbolic perspective, the Knower just knows what they know, but has nothing to prove or be noticed about. It's inner knowing, coupled with wisdom. It's complete trust and faith in their intuition. The heart connection is strong and leads the way.

LEADER

Tribal: At this level, the leader has to lead at all costs and must be seen to be in charge. It is similar to the Controller. The Leader does not want others to lead because that will mean they may not be in control. There's usually a lot of arrogance around the Leader and they can be egocentric. They want to hear how wonderful they are. It can also mean they won't lead because of the fear of getting it wrong and having to be accountable for their actions.

> *Ask Yourself: Do you always have to be in the lead and if so, why? Are you too frightened to step up and lead? Where does this come from What do you believe a true leader looks like anyway?*

Symbolic: The Leader at this level can step up and lead, but without the ego attachment. They are also happy to let others lead as well. They are totally capable of blending into the background. At this level, they listen to their Higher Self for guidance around leadership and come from a place of wisdom and discernment.

LOVER

Tribal: At this level, the Lover will often make everyone responsible for loving them. They may blame their partner when it doesn't work out and then move on hoping the next one will be better. This may happen many times and the trick is to see that you are the common denominator in these failed relationships.

They may also fear losing love, so will move on to make sure they don't get hurt. It can also mean that this person has a Disneyland version of being rescued by Prince Charming if they are female. If a male, he's waiting for his Princess to appear, who of course, will be perfect.

Another version of the Lover is the person who is shut down from loving, either the self or another, because of feeling so betrayed in the past, so refuses to let love in.

Ask Yourself: Are you open to loving yourself first before hoping another will truly love you? Do you understand that you can't expect another to love you if you dislike yourself on the inside? What is your role model for intimacy? Has it been a destructive one?

Are you safe to open up to love, of yourself, or of another? Are you willing to allow another to truly "see" you and love you, all of you?

Symbolic: The Lover at the Symbolic or Conscious level takes full responsibility for the self and understands the self-love component. Until one practices this, then they'll never attract in the partner they're truly wanting. They no longer project their needs onto others. They can take risks knowing it's better to have loved than not at all. The core self of love always remains intact as it comes from Pure Spirit. It's even understood that there's no such thing as a broken heart, only a broken ego and broken links to your Higher Self.

MAIDEN/MOTHER/CRONE

Tribal: This is the trilogy of the feminine journey through life. At the tribal level, the Maiden just wants everyone to still rescue her, and at the Individuation level, the mother does not want to give up mothering and certainly does not tend to herself. Depending on what level this archetype appears, tells you where you're stuck, be it the Tribal or Individuation levels.

The Masculine version of this is **_Knight/Father/Sage_**, but the same understanding applies except that the Knight has to keep on rescuing the damsel in distress.

> *Ask Yourself: Do you expect to always be rescued in your life? Do you find life too hard and just want someone to do it for you? If you're male do you have to rescue females from their different predicaments? What's the payoff here?*
>
> *At the* **Individuation** *level, why can't you let go of mothering or fathering? Is that what defines you?*

Symbolic: At this level, the Crone is in charge. There is now the wisdom to enjoy each stage of life and live without regrets, knowing everything has been part of the learning and remembering the truth of who you really are. Each age group brings its own special joys and growth, so there is no need to live in the past or wish life was another way. Acceptance and trust are the key words here.

The same goes for the Sage – he can live in the moment, without the need to rescue or save anyone as he trusts that everything is there for a reason. He truly likes himself and accepts what is.

MAGICIAN/SORCERER

Tribal: The Magician at this level can create magic but may refuse to do so, because of a deep fear of misusing power. Or the reverse, they use it only for self and not for the good of others. They may be cynical and judgmental, which will be a mask as they are frightened to step up to the plate and own who they are.

It may also be that the Magician uses it for everyone else, except for his or her own use. This way it is seen as helpful, but by not using it for themselves they can stay safe and righteous.

> *Ask Yourself: Do you create magic for yourself or only for others? Are you frightened to use your gifts because of what others may think of you? What's your definition of magic?*

Symbolic: Symbolically speaking, the Magician practices magic for the good of the whole and does not need the self-aggrandizement, therefore has no personal agenda. They know they can manifest whatever they want, be it for self or other, but they have no investment in doing so. The manifestation of magic is always for the highest good as they understand they always have their needs met and therefore nothing to prove.

MAIDEN/KNIGHT

Tribal: Tribally speaking, the Maiden does not know how to take care of herself and expects others to rescue her. The Knight loves to rescue and get the kudos for it. They both have to learn how to grow up.

This is another duality Archetype.

> *Ask Yourself: Do you love to rescue or be rescued? Do you take responsibility for others when it is not your place to do so and if so, why? If you're the maiden: Do you take responsibility for your own actions?*

Symbolic: At this level, it is associated with spiritual purity. The Maiden takes full responsibility for what she has created and gets on with it. The Knight understands he rescues others when his heart directs him to do it, but not as an avoidance technique regarding dealing with his own issues.

MASCOT

Tribal: The Mascot, at this level, has no idea who they really are, so becomes the Chameleon and does what everyone else wants them to do. They adapt their roles according to whom they are with. The challenge is to KNOW THYSELF.

> *Ask Yourself: Whom or what do you fear losing if you become yourself? Why is it so hard to claim your own individuality? What's the payoff for not being true to yourself?*

Symbolic: The Mascot, at this level, has clear boundaries in place and has developed good self worth and esteem. They are able to speak their truth clearly, as their own integrity is important to them. The inner self matches the outer self; there is no difference between the two. What you see is what you get.

MAVERICK

Tribal: This person shoots "from the lip" instead of "shooting from the hip" (this goes back to an old TV program called Maverick who was a gun slinger turned lawman). They hide behind their cutting comments by saying: ... well, it's the truth and only your best friend would tell you...(doesn't matter that it's hurtful.)

They often have a hidden agenda in what they're saying and can use words in a very manipulative manner. It can be similar to the Philosopher at the Tribal level.

> *Ask Yourself:* Do you use words to manipulate and control others? Do you speak without thinking of the consequences? Are you righteous in believing your way is the only way?

Symbolic: At this level, the Maverick Archetype knows the importance of what words come out of the mouth as they carry a resonance or a vibration. Therefore, they choose to use words that are couched in wisdom and love, while always speaking their truth. Symbolically speaking, the Maverick will say what others are afraid to say, but it comes from the heart, not ego.

MARTYR

Tribal: This is a dangerous archetype at the tribal level as it leads to many illnesses. People usually need a role model to learn how to be the Martyr, so it may be one of your parents that taught you how to play this role.

They tend to SIGH a lot at this level, meaning, "If you only knew how much I give up for you or do for you," and so on. They do not live for themselves, but vicariously through others. They often exhaust themselves and do not have clear boundaries.

> Ask Yourself: What price do you pay for being a Martyr? Why do you play this role? Who was your role model for this? Does it serve you? How have you played Martyr in the past?

Symbolic: The Martyr sees the futility in playing this role, so stops suffering and lives in joy and from the heart. They are now true to the self and no longer need others to acknowledge their actions. They become fully responsible for their own well being and live in their integrity.

MIDAS

Tribal: Very few people have a right relationship to money as we're subliminally taught that it's God. It's easy to have a great relationship to money when you have plenty of it, but when it's not abundant the truth really kicks in. It is a false God and most people live in fear of not having enough or of losing what they do have.

The Midas touch can also be the person who has the knack of

everything working out well, no matter what they do. But at this level, there is fear of taking the risk and trusting themselves. Pay attention if this shows up in the second or eighth Houses as it is directly related to the issue of money.

> *Ask Yourself: Where did you get your beliefs around money? Are they fear based ones? Do they serve you? Are you living in fear of not having enough money? Do you take responsibility and cut your cloth according to what you have, or do you expect to have everything even when you can't pay for it? If so, where does this come from?*
>
> *What are your beliefs around abundance in general? Do you use money to compensate for other areas in your life that are lacking in joy?*

Symbolic: At this level, you're straight with money, not in fear of it anymore. You know you can manifest whatever you need. You understand that money is just energy and every bit as available to you as your next breath. You trust the Divine process of abundance. You do not believe the world owes you a living, but see it as the game it really is. You are willing to work hard because work is a joy and passion. However, it can also come easily as well, without working hard if that is what is important to you.

If someone has the Midas touch, then they enjoy doing this for the good of the whole. It usually means the person is good at manifesting his or her own reality.

Abundance at this level means it is across the board: physical, mental, emotional, and spiritual as well as financial abundance.

MONK/NUN

Tribal: This person believes they can only get to God through a third party, be it the priest, rabbi or minister. They see "God" as still outside of themselves and often have a parent/child relationship to God because that's what they've been taught.

It's usually lifetimes old. It may also mean they have served God many times, vowing poverty and chastity. Now when they have to learn self love and empowerment, they get very confused. The old lessons of subservience are still very strong at the subconscious level. Plus, who are they without the Church's rules?

It carries similar energy to the Disciple. It is also a duality Archetype, representing a version of the masculine/feminine within, but usually from a spiritual perspective.

> *Ask Yourself: Do you believe that "God" is an external authority in your life? Are you only valid if you're living in poverty and serving others? Can you easily allow joy into your life on a personal level or does it always have to be seen to be "spiritual?" Do you put others down if they live a life of abundance and happiness?*

Symbolic: The Monk/Nun at this level does not need a church or an Order to get to God, as they understand THEY ARE GOD in human form. There is no longer any separation. They have reclaimed their power back from the manipulated thinking they were given. They understand that everything arises in the Divine Condition - everything. There is no such thing as "getting back to God" because they never left in the first place.

MOTHER/FATHER

Tribal: This may be the abusive mother or father who neglects his or her responsibilities. It may also be the parent who does not know how to give emotionally. There is no physical bonding or touching. This Archetype may give the child money but not be present at all in the relationship because they're too busy making money. This parent may believe that as long as material needs are met, then they have fulfilled their role as a parent.

It could also be the over protective parent who can never let go of their child. A common term these days is the "helicopter" parent who is always hovering over their child. One does not need to have children to pull this archetype.

It can also include Mother Earth at the unconscious level, meaning the one who supplies all our needs, such as food, air, heat and water.

It is another duality Archetype and may mean that there is a huge split between the mind and the heart or the left-brain and right brain.

If this Archetype appears in the fourth or tenth houses, pay attention as the fourth house is the house of the Mother and the tenth house is the house of the Father. It's giving you an important message.

> *Ask Yourself: Are you totally in your mind? Does your heart get a look in? Are you repeating roles that you hated when you were a child and giving them to your own children? Are you present with your children, or do you just give them money so they don't bother you? How connected are you with your own inner child?*

Do you always have to be the Authority figure, proving you're right all the time? Are you safe enough to simply listen to your child, literally (as well as your own inner child)? Do you always have to fix them or tell them what they need to do next? Do you negate their feelings and shame them?

Do you forget to give gratitude to the Earth Mother for all that she gives you?

Symbolic: Here, the parent is totally present and conscious regarding their nurturing role. This parent is available at all levels to their own children, and also to their Child within. They understand there's no such thing as the perfect parent or the perfect child, as they do not exist, so they simply do the best job they know how.

It can also symbolically represent the marriage of the masculine and feminine within or the yin/yang component of self.

MYSTIC

Tribal: This Archetype can mean that you have a very hard pathway to walk as you've come here to learn how to be in the world, but not of the world. It means that you have a certain knowledge or understanding of energy and how it works, but do not trust this yet.

The fear may be that once you get on this pathway, there's no getting off. The monkey mind plays tricks and says, "What will be asked of me, and what will I have to give up? Will it mean leaving my Tribe behind and setting out on a solitary journey?"

This fear can translate into feeling very alone and isolated, but this is the illusion. It's a nebulous Archetype as it's hard to define.

> *Ask Yourself:* Are you listening to your heart or are you being ruled by logic and mind? What do you know internally but are afraid to own? Do you get a sense of a higher purpose but you're afraid to trust it? Is there fear from within about stepping out on a different pathway to everyone else?

Symbolic: Here the Mystic seeks understanding and union with Source. At this level, usually the dark night of the soul has been undertaken, perhaps through ill health, financial issues, political violence and so forth. They see the illusion for what it is and move through it and learn to live in the world, but not be of the world.

The trick is to see everything as connected to Source, knowing that you have come here to experience duality, which means taking both positive and negative experiences as just that - experiences. You stop putting labels on things and just go with the experience knowing it's all part of the Divine process.

MYTH

Tribal: This can be a dangerous Archetype at this level, as it can lead to all sorts of bowel or gut problems. This person totally holds onto their past, via anger, vengeance, regret, shame, bitterness or guilt instead of healing the past and letting it go.

You can inherit someone else's Myth or past as well, especially if your culture teaches you to hate others or see others as inferior or dangerous to you.

Ask Yourself: What are you holding onto about your past? What is it that you can't let go of and why? What's the pay off? Do you get to stay "safe and righteous" by blaming others all the time?

Symbolic: Here, the Myth Archetype has learned to face their past, heal it, forgive it and let it go. They understand the lesson of forgiveness and realize that it was all self created.

If you're here to learn about forgiveness, then you usually have to find something really big to forgive, so in comes betrayal, rejection and abandonment. It's the journey of the Christ Consciousness into forgiveness and emerging out of the darkness and seeing that we're all connected in some way or another. At the end of the day, every human being just wants to be loved.

OBSERVER

Tribal: The Observer likes to sit on the fence because the fear is they will mess up if they take action. The belief is that they may not be good enough, clever enough and strong enough. Will they have what it takes to succeed at a role or a new venture? So rather than test themselves, they don't take risks and stay safe by not doing anything. The trouble is that a lot of life passes them by because fear calls the shots. The Procrastinator can walk hand in hand with this Archetype.

Ask Yourself: What or who are you afraid of? Do you lack self-confidence and self worth? If so, where did you learn this? Do you believe in yourself?

Symbolic: At this level, the Observer learns to live life to the fullest. They no longer fear getting it wrong because they have learned how to trust in their inner guidance. They don't buy into right/wrong and instead, understand it's all about the experience. Right and wrong sit in the Tribal level, as it's a man made belief. At the Symbolic level, it's about the journey and the experience, not about winning or losing.

OLYMPIAN

Tribal: The lesson here is to learn endurance, strength, discipline, commitment, fortitude, and the ability to go the distance or the extra mile, using your stamina and resilience. This can be applied to all walks of life, not just the sporting field.

At this level, the Olympian is all about winning and being number one as well as getting the gold medal and the accolades that go with it.

> *Ask Yourself: Why do you need to win all the time and what lengths will you go to, to make sure you win? Do you get a huge sense of achievement from winning? Who are you if you don't win? Or do you lack discipline and commitment in your life? Does this lack of discipline come from the belief that it's too hard? Where did you learn this?*

Symbolic: At this level, the lessons are learned and integrated. You accept your Personal Best, knowing you've done all you could to run this race, no matter what area of life this relates to. You no longer need the accolades that go with winning and you no longer compare yourself to others. You understand the deeper truth that it's how you run the race that matters, not getting the gold medal. You know inner peace.

OTHER DIMENSIONS

Tribal: This person is in fear of opening themselves up psychically and exploring other realms. There's usually a karmic memory that says they will be killed if they start exploring beyond the physical. It's not rational of course, just experienced in the form of fear of the unknown. They are often fascinated by it, but also terrified by it, so stay safe by looking on from a distance.

> *Ask Yourself: What will happen to you if you start exploring other ways of being? Will you get caught up in a cult? Will you be taken over by other energies? What latent gifts do you have that you're too frightened to own? Do you remember seeing spirit beings when you were a child? Were you told this was all in your imagination?*

Symbolic: The fears no longer exist as they've been confronted and absolved. At this level, you see the Oneness in everything, no matter the form. You now have an intimate and personal knowledge of Other Dimensions and can speak from experience as opposed to head knowledge. You understand you are a Multi Dimensional Being, existing simultaneously on many levels of Awareness.

PAN

Tribal: This person needs to get into Nature to heal and balance, however ironically, they never seem to get there. Their intentions are good, but always sabotaged in some way. Yet they often have a profound love of Nature itself. The best way to utilize the Archetype of Pan is to ask for help from Nature, to heal the current imbalance and learn how to let the natural forces do this.

It's best if one is in a high-energy spot like the forest, mountains or the beach, but even your own back garden will do. You ask the Devas of the trees to come and help in the healing process to restore you to balance and harmony. Then simply sit still and just BE.

> *Ask Yourself:* Do you get out into Nature as often as you would like? If not, why? How do you sabotage yourself from making this happen? How do you feel when you're in Nature and just soaking it all up? Do you feel connected when you're in Nature, centered and more balanced?

Symbolic: At this level, you can call Pan to serve and heal you, while sitting in your lounge room chair. Your connection with Gaia/Pan is very strong and you know how to call this energy in to help heal and balance. Ironically, you don't have to physically go out into Nature. Your connection is so strong at this level that Nature will come to you. You can commune with Pan no matter where you are because you understand that Nature is part of the Oneness and just another expression of the Divine Condition.

PEACEMAKER/STATESPERSON

Tribal: This is an "umbrella" archetype for many other Archetypes. From this role of the Peacemaker come many others such as good girl, mascot, clown/fool, healer, rescuer and so on.

The deepest fear of the Peacemaker is conflict, so they will do anything to avoid it, hence needing to play all the other roles.

They usually have strong childhood memories of being frightened because of abuse, shouting, violence or arguments. These memories bring up their fear of being out of control and therefore not safe. So the Peacemaker plays roles to make sure everything stays peaceful around them, but at a huge cost to the self.

Ask Yourself: How does the Peacemaker play out in your life? Why are you frightened of conflict? Do you have inner peace? Do you speak your truth at all times and if not, what's the belief that tells you you're not safe to do this? How can you bring more peace into your life, both inner and outer?

Symbolic: At this level, the Peacemaker wants peace, on all levels, but from the highest level, and for the good of the whole. They are no longer frightened of conflict, seeing it as a difference in perspective and not a right or wrong.

This Archetype at the symbolic level is typified by Gandhi, who wanted peace and independence for India and got it, but by peaceful means. Being at peace means being in integrity and authentic and you will not be compromised, but you achieve this from your heart's guidance, not from the mind.

PERFECTIONIST

Tribal: This is another dangerous archetype at the tribal level as it can lead to illness, particularly migraines and allergies. This person believes they have to be perfect at everything. They must be at the top of the class, as that's the way to stay safe and in control. They don't need any outside enemies as their own internal enemy (the mind and its beliefs) does all the damage. It's a learned behavioral pattern from childhood to win approval from authority figures and therefore "stay safe."

Ask Yourself: Whose voice is it that's telling you to be perfect? Is it your mother, your father, or your culture? How much does this voice run your life? Does it bring you deep peace and joy? Do you feel stressed because of this voice?

Symbolic: At this level, the Perfectionist has learned the balance, as they no longer seek outside approval. They see the cosmic humor by realizing that everything is perfectly imperfect. They know when to let go and walk away. They understand that at the tribal level, the motivation is fear. Instead, at the symbolic level, personal best is enough. Inner peace is gained as the connection is now with the heart, not the mind.

PHILOSOPHER

Tribal: The Philosopher at the tribal level needs to be validated for their mind and intellect. They may use mind to feel superior to others as they often feel disconnected from their own emotional body and feelings. With this person, only mind exists, along with the practical, scientific reality that validates any argument that may arise. This person may be good at manipulating language and skilled at making another look foolish.

Ask Yourself: Do you use your mind to impress others or to manipulate so that you get what you want? Do you only use your mind, to the detriment of your heart? Do you ignore your feelings and emotions? Are you sensitive to other people's feelings or don't you care about anyone else?

Symbolic: At the symbolic level the Philosopher no longer needs to impress. They may have a lot of knowledge but no longer need to flaunt it. Paradoxically, they understand the more they know, the less they know.

At this level, the Philosopher is able to surrender to the Divine Mind because they trust that whatever they need to know will drop in. It is understood that there's a vast difference between the Divine Mind and the Human Mind. The latter is used by the ego to feel superior. At this level, the ego no longer calls the shots. The heart is in charge.

PIONEER

Tribal: The Pioneer Archetype loves finding new pathways, but it can be used as a distraction and avoidance when not wanting to deal with challenging issues. They may walk where others fear to tread however and can get a high from the adrenalin rush that goes with new adventures.

It can also mean that they know they should start out on a new pathway but old fears and beliefs keep them stuck doing the same old thing.

> *Ask Yourself: Are you too frightened to walk a new pathway so stay safe by doing what you've always done? What's your motivation for always exploring new territories? Do you love the thrill of being first to find something new?*

Symbolic: The Pioneer at this level faces the unknown but also takes care of business across the board. They are in touch with their intuition by listening to their internal guidance and feel divinely led. They do not need the gilt edged guarantee before they step into new territory, as they know the proof will drop in afterwards if needed. They have learned how to listen to their heart and then use the mind to give them the practicalities they need to implement a new journey.

PRINCE/PRINCESS

Tribal: This person expects royal treatment all the time, but never seems to be able to step up to the plate to get the job done themselves. Instead they want someone else to do it for them or with them. They would love someone else to come in and take care of business. They are usually not interested in learning how to get their hands dirty, or to acquire a new skill. Rather, they would love to command that someone else does the job for them.

This is one of the duality Archetypes, so metaphysically speaking it's asking, "Is my head calling the shots all the time? Where's my heart's guidance?"

> *Ask Yourself: How lazy are you or is there a part of you that just wants someone else to do it for you? Why do you want things handed to you on a platter all the time? Do you have an entitlement issue that says you should be able to have it all, without working for any of it?*

Symbolic: At this level, they have become grounded and real and will do what it takes to get the business done. They are still capable of enjoying the good things in life. They no longer expect others to serve them, as they are happy to get their hands dirty if it means completing a task. The right brain and left-brain talk easily to each other and live in harmony.

PROCRASTINATOR

Tribal: This Archetype has a fear of getting it wrong or making a mistake, so refuses to make a decision. They often wish someone else would make the decision for them. They specialize in the mind going "will I/won't I" and it can drive them insane. It's time to examine the motivation behind the fear.

> *Ask Yourself:* Why are you paralyzed when it comes to making decisions in your life? What's behind this fear? How does it serve you to keep this fear going?

Symbolic: The Procrastinator realizes they are just putting off learning their lessons, so they examine the fear behind it. This enables them to make decisions and accept the consequences as they learn about life and fear induced programming. They dispel the illusion around the fear and step into their highest potential.

PROPHET/VISIONARY

Tribal: Two Archetypes in one. The Prophet and the Visionary. With both of these attributes at the tribal level, you must have validation of your prophecy or your vision. You do not trust yourself and the fear is what if it's wrong? It's not understood that the point of Prophecy is that it's not meant to come true. Enough people are meant to receive the prophecy to bring about change. However, the skeptic says unless it happens, it was not true in the first place. The point of the Visionary is to hold the vision in spite of what others tell them.

It can also mean that a person is gifted in this area but is too frightened to implement it because of what others will say. It may be that old memory says you'll be ridiculed in some way if you share your prophecy or vision. This Archetype is often aligned with the Square Peg in the Round Hole.

> *Ask Yourself: Do you trust your intuition or inner knowing? Do you need validation from others before you know it to be true? What will be asked of you if you claim this ability and start to use it? How will your life change?*

Symbolic: At this level, the Prophet/Visionary can hold the vision or prophecy, trusting in their own higher guidance and heart's direction. They don't care what others say, nor do they need to be right. They can act on their dreams and visions and stand in their integrity. They do not mind standing alone and separate from the Tribe. Their own heart's truth keeps them in harmony and balance. At this level, they align with the Mystic and work for the good of the whole.

PROTECTOR

Tribal: This energy is similar to the Controller. There is a strong need to protect loved ones, as the Controller does not believe people can look after themselves. A level of arrogance comes in here. No one else can do the job as well as they can.

It can also mean that through the fear of not feeling safe, this Archetype will call in someone to protect him or her and totally give his or her power away to this other person. This keeps them safe at the tribal level as they get to blame the other person if something goes wrong.

> *Ask Yourself: Why do you not feel safe unless you're*

protecting everything around you? Do you need others to protect you, as you feel incapable of looking after yourself? What will happen to you if you're not in control all the time, or not being protected? How will your world fall apart?

Symbolic: The Protector can now trust and let go for they understand they're safe as their power comes from within. They can trust others to take care of themselves and understand that they have called in their experiences for their growth. They support but do not control.

PUCK

Tribal: This person is always cracking jokes – so that others will see them as funny. If you challenge the Puck person's humor, they'll tell you to get a life. They like to be the joke teller. They do not like being at the receiving end of someone else's joke.

They often make a joke at someone else's expense.

Puck humor can be used as a way to avoid conflict or defuse a situation

Puck is a Shakespearean term so not commonly known, but archetypally, at the tribal level, it's about not understanding that what goes around, comes around, so playing jokes on others or hiding behind a joke will backfire one day.

Ask Yourself: Do you hide behind your jokes rather than speak your truth clearly? Do you find it funny to make jokes about other people and if so, why? Are you okay with being the butt of someone else's joke? Can you hand it out but not take it?

What is going on in your life right now that means a joke could backfire on you? Where did you learn to crack jokes all the time? Is it annoying to others and you don't realize it?

Symbolic: At this level, the Puck person has learned to take responsibility for his or her language and emotions. They no longer need to poke fun at anyone else. Archetypally it means that the joke no longer needs to backfire, it's been diffused because Consciousness now calls the shots. They understand the Law of Reciprocity, meaning what goes around comes around.

REBEL

Tribal: The Rebel Archetype refuses to accept the status quo, therefore has to fight against the law and authority figures. They can carry a big chip on their shoulder about injustice and inequality. This often relates back to their childhood or culture and how they were treated. They may have temper tantrums if it's at the Tribal level, but at the Individuation level, it's rebelling like a teenager so defying authority figures.

Ask Yourself: What are you really rebelling about? What deep-seated feelings are still inside that you haven't addressed? Why do you resent authority figures? What has happened to you in the past that make you feel this way?

Symbolic: The Rebel has learned how to take responsibility for their own actions and can now march to the beat of their own drum. They no longer have a chip on their shoulder as they can see the bigger picture, so they deal with their own issues and take responsibility for their feelings and actions. At this level, they understand the pain behind the need to rebel and if rebellion is still needed, it's done so for the highest good of all.

RESCUER

Tribal: The Rescuer Archetype often has a hidden agenda, as they want to be valued and needed by others. Quite often they're very busy rescuing others, but never themselves, as they don't have any energy left. This is avoidance and denial. Arrogance comes into the picture too, because of the belief that no one else can do the job but him or her.

> *Ask Yourself: Do you rescue others a lot and if so, why? Is it to avoid dealing with your own issues? Do you believe that no one else will do the job as well as you can? What kudos do you love receiving from always rescuing others? Do you feel special?*

Symbolic: At the Symbolic level, the Rescuer stops rescuing others and works on their own healing instead. They no longer need others to validate them and tell them how wonderful they are because of all that they do. If they do rescue at this level, they equally do the same amount of work on the self, so there's no longer avoidance going on.

RISK TAKER

Tribal: This person talks a lot, but rarely takes actions. Instead, fear calls the shots so they stay safe doing what they've always done. They'll encourage others to take risks, but when it comes to the self, it's in the too hard basket.

It can also mean that this person does indeed take risks, but there's no wisdom behind them, they are knee jerk reactions instead.

It could be an attitudinal shift that needs to happen as well, like taking a risk with changing perceptions and beliefs.

> *Ask Yourself: Why are you too frightened to make changes in your life? Do you act in a foolhardy manner and live to regret it? Do you talk about doing things, but never seem to step out of your comfort zone?*

Symbolic: The Risk Taker understands fear is a game used by the ego/mind to stop change happening. This person uses wisdom to evaluate a situation and examine it from all angles. They see the bigger picture and understand why they have called a situation in as it's for their own growth. At this level, they feel the fear and do it anyway, once it feels right from the heart's perspective.

SAGE/CRONE

Tribal: By definition, one cannot move into the Sage/Crone archetype until over fifty because it's about wisdom and maturity. However, there are some children who are five, going on fifty. The Sage/Crone may have to move away from their family to learn wisdom through initiation. But at this level, they are frightened of their own wisdom and intuition, because they don't know how to trust it and usually don't listen to it.

This is one of the duality Archetypes, so therefore it's also about the balance between the masculine/feminine connection or left brain/right brain competition.

> *Ask Yourself: Are you safe to trust your inner wisdom and if*

not, why not? Who has told you it's not safe to listen within? What price do you put on wisdom? Do you value other's wisdom rather than your own? Why?

Symbolic: Symbolically, the Sage/Crone has matured into the wise man/woman. Wisdom is leading as opposed to intelligence, or another way to put this, is that the heart has come to the fore and is used in conjunction with the mind. Another name for the Sage/Crone may also be a Seer, who sees with internal spiritual eyes, as well as with the external eyes.

SCAPEGOAT

Tribal: A tricky Archetype as they feel victimized and believe that everyone is out to get them. This may include family members or in a work situation. They feel others dump on them. At this Tribal level, the Unconscious works out that any attention is worthwhile, even if it's negative! At an unseen level, the Scapegoat seems to wear an invisible sign that says, "Come and dump on me, blame me or tell me I'm wrong all the time!"

> *Ask Yourself: What's the carrot here when you play this role? Is there a better way to be noticed or to ask for your needs to be met? When did you start this sort of behavior or have you always felt this way? Does it serve you to keep playing this role? How are you scapegoating yourself?*

Symbolic: At this level of awareness, the Scapegoat understands it's a role they've chosen to play and that this can change. They do have a choice. They no longer act out everyone's negative side and choose empowerment instead. His or her self worth and self-esteem is now in place and therefore they refuse to be dumped on.

SCHOLAR

Tribal: The Scholar Archetype may become the eternal student, as they're always learning, but not integrating or living it. They may be addicted to the academic system and need a lot of certificates and degrees to tell them they're okay. They always feel like they have more to learn and it's always external learning from other authority figures.

> *Ask Yourself: How does being the Student all the time stop you from going within and trusting yourself? Why do you feel you're never going to have enough knowledge? Do you believe that the mind will validate you and keep you safe in the outside world? Is this a strategy that stops you from going and living you truth in the outside world?*

Symbolic: At the symbolic level, the Student allows for integration, absorbs it on all levels, values their knowledge but doesn't get off on it. They're not frightened to go out and explore life as they live it rather than learn or read about it. They also understand that the deepest truth comes from the heart, not the mind.

SCRIBE REPORTER

Tribal: The Scribe Reporter may hide behind writing and may fantasize about life. They may not report accurately about things. They may sensationalize headlines or articles. Behind this is the need to be validated or noticed. There's an agenda about receiving the accolades and earning the praise.

Or they may want to write but not feel good enough to put pen to paper. They could sabotage themselves all the time with not allowing the space for this to happen. Perhaps the excuse is that I have too many things to do before I can allow myself this level of pleasure.

> *Ask Yourself: Do you yearn to write and won't give yourself the time to do it? Do you use the written word to manipulate and cajole? Can you let go and allow your feelings and thoughts to flow and pour out of you, onto paper?*

Symbolic: At this level, the Scribe reports without bias and allows for Divine Guidance to flow through and take over. They are able to tell the higher story, as it's coming from the heart instead of the mind. They write without agendas or simply for their own pleasure, joy and creativity.

SEARCHER

Tribal: The Searcher always believes there's more. What's the next teacher/course/workshop that I have to do to learn more, as I don't know enough? There is no trust in their inner guidance or wisdom. They've been taught it's always outside of them. It can also mean that they love the search, indeed can become addicted to it, but may not necessarily want the truth.

> *Ask Yourself: Why are you always searching outside of yourself for someone else's truth? Are you prepared to search inside for your answers? Is searching all the time a way of avoiding getting to know yourself more?*

Symbolic: At this level, the Searcher stops the search,

because everything they've ever needed to know is already inside. They surrender into trust and faith because they understand that the next step will reveal itself. They open up to their intuition and inner higher guidance.

SERVANT

Tribal: The Servant may have resentment towards their job be it paid employment or in the home. It can feel unfulfilling for them. They can believe that others have it much easier than they do and can play the victim. Hating the job you're doing and feeling the energy of resentment all day long may lead to illness further on down the track. The Servant at this level finds it easier to feel envy of others rather than do anything about their current situation.

> *Ask Yourself*: *What or who do you resent serving? Why? Are you willing to make change happen so that you can move this attitude?*

Symbolic: The Servant understands they create their own reality and will serve out of the joy of it rather than the drudgery. It's understood that being the Servant is a mindset, not a prison sentence. It may possibly even lead to Sainthood, as at this level, the highest good for all is the motivation.

SHAMAN

Tribal: The Shaman used to be seen as the Witch Doctor or Medicine Man and had the ability to commune with Nature and talk to the Spirits of the Trees and Animals.

These days, it may play out with the Shaman knowing they

have abilities but won't use them. They are too fear based around what others will think of them. They retain old memory about consequences from other lifetimes around what may happen if they step up to the plate and own their unique skills and talents.

They may not know how to activate their skills, because of this fear. It may also be that they use their shamanic gifts of transformation to help others, but not themselves. Another possibility is that they use their gifts for their own agenda and in the process often hurt others.

A Shamanic experience can be recovering from cancer, a massive heart attack or a stroke. It may be coming back from huge financial loss, or a devastating fire. The Shamanic journey is about transformation.

> *Ask Yourself: Do you have gifts or talents that you hide and if so, why? Do you use your talents only for your own desires and justify this in the process? Have you got the internal courage to make the necessary transformation of your current, untenable situation?*

Symbolic: At this level of awareness, there is no fear left, just trust. To get to this point, one usually has to go through a rite of passage, some form of near death experience or a dark night of the soul. It's Harry Potter fighting Voldemort! There usually needs to be a deep connection to Nature as well, as this energy works with all forms of expression.

The Shaman does not feel victimized by his or her situation, but understands it was for growth so that they could make the necessary transformation. It may be in the physical or with the mind and therefore realize their deepest truth in their own heart.

SLAVE

Tribal: The Slave has similar characteristics to the Servant, but with a greater sense of victimhood. They can feel totally powerless because of the situation they find themselves in. This may be physical or mental. This energy of the Slave at this level can mean addictions in many forms, be it drugs, hard work, food, depression, gambling, controlling others, violence, attitudes and behaviors and so forth.

> *Ask Yourself: What are you a slave to in your physical world? Do you hold onto rigid perceptions? How does this work for you? Do you hide behind your addictions so that you don't have to step up to the plate and be counted?*

Symbolic: The Slave has taken their power back and overcome the addiction to powerlessness and therefore restores their sense of self worth and respect. At this level, they reclaim their Sovereignty. It is understood they are no-one's slave, as they realize it's about attitude. This comes from changing perceptions about life.

SQUARE PEG IN ROUND HOLE

Tribal: I created this Archetype as I saw it in so many people's energy field. It means the person usually feels different to everyone else and they can often apologize for those differences. It can be considered another "umbrella" archetype, playing out as the good girl/boy, rescuer, helper, servant and others.

Many children feel like this, as they know they have unique talents but choose not to use them to keep other people safe in their family or with their peer group. This means that they dumb themselves down to be accepted and be considered "normal." They simply don't feel like they fit in and it's true, they don't. They are different to the Tribe but as a child, they have no idea how to express those differences or even feel safe to share them.

> *Ask Yourself:* How different do you feel and are you safe to explore those differences? What needs to happen to change this around? Is it time to stop apologizing for the uniqueness of who you are? Can you accept yourself as enough, knowing you're doing the best job you know how?

Symbolic: At this level, the Square Peg no longer apologizes for their differences, but revels in the fact that they are different. They know the Divine doesn't make mistakes and whoever they are is perfect for their journey this time around. They no longer feel separate, but value the differences as the unique expression of the many faces of Source energy. They trust in their own inner guidance and feel very comfortable in their own skin.

STORYTELLER

Tribal: At this level, the Storyteller may have the gift of the gab, but usually exaggerates the story to gain more impact. They never let the truth get in the way of a good ending. It may also be that because of a painful childhood, the Storyteller lives in his or her own fantasy story, as it's not safe to live in the "real" world.

Ask Yourself: What story do you tell yourself that is fear based and not the truth? How do you keep your old story alive? Do you tell your story over and over again to anyone who will listen? Do you want to change the old story and if so, what stops you from doing it?

Symbolic: At this level, the Storyteller uses their gifts to tell the Divine Story. They no longer need to exaggerate, they simply tell it how it is, as they no longer need to impress others. They see the bigger picture and can separate out the fantasy from the higher reality. Their heart now calls the shots instead of the mind's projections and perceptions.

TEACHER

Tribal: The Teacher Archetype often likes to feel superior to their students and must have more knowledge than them. They need to be seen as the authority figure. It may also mean that they are stuck in the teaching profession, which no longer holds any passion for them, but they are just there to pick up a salary at the end of the week. They do not understand that the teacher/pupil archetype is symbiotic. They need each other and can learn from one other.

It may also mean that you have things to teach, but do not feel "qualified" or fear being "out there" because of what others may think.

Ask Yourself: What are you teaching that no longer feels right for you? Do you still have passion for this work? What could you be teaching but are too frightened to do so? Whose approval do you still need?

Symbolic: At this level of awareness, the Teacher stays open minded, ethical and willing to learn. They can be inspirational and influence others for their highest good. They understand that everyone learns from each other. They understand they will never know it all, so they teach from their own heart's truth as well as from the intellect. They live their teachings and it shows.

TRANSITION

Tribal: This Archetype knows that they're at a crossroads, but feels too frightened to take the next step. They want the gilt edged guarantee that they'll be safe before they'll move on. It's only the mind that is stuck in an old pattern of fear based thinking, but at this level, it feels hard to shift. They would love someone to hold their hand as they make the next move.

> *Ask Yourself: What changes do you need to make in your life and what stops you from making them? What do you believe will happen if you make a move and it doesn't turn out? Whose support do you need or have you got enough courage to do it on your own?*

Symbolic: The Transition Archetype feels the fear and does it anyway. They understand that fear is a trick of the ego or Saboteur to keep them from achieving their highest potential. At this level, they can trust in their intuition and their inner guidance so can easily move to make the necessary changes in their life. We're always transitioning from one level of awareness to another. It's called the game of life!

TRICKSTER

Tribal: This may be the used car salesman that knows they're selling you a car full of rust, or the real estate guy that knows the house is full of white ants. What they don't get is what goes around, comes around. They usually don't like it when they at the receiving end of a trick, as they will not own the mirror that this is what they do to others.

The Tribal level represents the physical, so it may be that you're playing a game with yourself somehow or other in your physical world. It may be that your mind is tricking you, believing in things that simply no longer serve you.

> *Ask Yourself: How are you tricking yourself? What stops you from paying attention to your intuition or heart? Do you only believe in the mind and its power? What foolish games do you play on others or yourself?*

Symbolic: At this level, the Trickster understands the game and how to play it, without taking it too seriously. They will not hurt or take advantage of others as they take full responsibility for their own actions. They understand that all of life is a game at some level, but it's what you do and your attitude to life that really matters. All is honored equally. They understand that what goes around, comes around.

TRUTH SEEKER

Tribal: The Truth Seeker wants the truth but only partially. There's internal bargaining going on that says, "Give me the truth in a way that I can handle. Don't challenge me too much, or interrupt my lifestyle. Give it to me in bits and pieces so that

I can cope and not be out of my comfort zone." The problem is that the Higher Self does not work this way. It wants you to trust first and walk the path of truth, then the proof drops in afterwards, but not before!

> *Ask Yourself:* What truth are you avoiding in yourself that is uncomfortable for you to own? Do you say you want the truth, but you really don't? Are you fearful that if you know the whole truth, it will change your life radically?

Symbolic: At this level, the word "truth" is interchangeable with God, Light, Love, Wisdom, Joy, Honour, Integrity - it no longer bargains for anything, just wants to live IN truth and AS truth. So no compromises are made, as authenticity, openness and being totally real become the only way to go.

VILLAIN CROOK

Tribal: This represents a sociopathic personality who has no social conscience. They often mix with very Tribal people who mirror each other and may enjoy making others suffer in some way. When I used to get people to choose their cards consciously, it was the least chosen Archetype! This is all about ripping others off and totally justifying why you do this.

> *Ask Yourself:* How are you ripping yourself off? Where is it playing out in your world? Is it in your physical world or maybe in your thinking? Are you being in integrity with your partner? Do you make shady deals financially and not find anything questionable about this? Do you take advantage of others, on any level?

Symbolic: At this level, you understand if you've been

ripped off, then it's time to look in the mirror and see what you're doing to yourself? If you've ever been robbed, then there is a need to ask how am I robbing myself, so at this level, you have the courage to ask these important questions. At this level, you take full responsibility for your actions, as you understand the Law of Reciprocity and you choose to live in honour and integrity. You do not rip yourself off, or others.

WANDERER

Tribal: The Wanderer wanders away either physically or mentally to avoid dealing with unpleasant situations. They're often not grounded and the expression, "the lights are on and no-one is home" can apply here. We can wander off physically, emotionally or mentally, as we're simply not present, maybe not even in our bodies but off somewhere else in fantasyland.

> *Ask Yourself: Why do you wander off physically, mentally or emotionally? What are you not dealing with? How does this serve you?*

Symbolic: The Wanderer realizes that they take their beliefs and mind with them, so there's no escaping the eventual truth. They choose to deal with reality and be totally present to all experiences. At this level of awareness however, you can choose to be the Wanderer, but not even leave your own home because you can tap into higher dimensions and commune with Spirit. You are no longer running from anything as your heart is connected to a deeper understanding of who you really are.

WARRIOR

Tribal: The Warrior loves to get into battle, if not their own, then someone else's, as they get off on winning and being the victor. They need to constantly prove their own power, however it's exhausting on all levels. It may be played out in the physical realms, but it could happen on the mental level as well as the emotional one. They love the high of winning, the adrenalin rush of being victorious. It becomes an addiction for many.

> *Ask Yourself: Do you have a lot of battles in your life and if so, why? Are they physical, mental or emotional ones? What thrill do you get when you win? Is it addictive? Do you look for battles to fight so that you can win and feel good? Are they your battles or someone else's?*

Symbolic: At this level, the Warrior gives up the battle, drops into the heart and listens to the highest truth. There is nothing to win, nothing to prove anymore, there is no competition as it's just the journey of the heart. They relinquish the battle and choose deep peace instead.

WEAVER

Tribal: This person has the skills to pull things together and make a new start, but chooses not to, because they don't believe in themselves. They may also want someone else to do it for them. So at the Tribal level, you're being asked to do what it takes to make change in your life. It's saying that you have everything within you that is needed to take the next step. But fear arises and starts to call the shots.

> *Ask Yourself: What stops you from weaving together all your*

skills so that change can happen? Where is your self worth
and self-esteem? Do you believe in yourself? If not, why?

Symbolic: At this level, they trust in themselves and their inner creativity. The Weaver listens to their higher self and follows the guidance to create a new beginning. They understand that all the new doorways will open if they trust and come from their heart.

WIZARD GENIUS

Tribal: This Archetype knows they can make a difference but fear overrides their inner knowing. They don't believe they are good enough, or else they are fearful of what will others think. It may also be that the Wizard Genius does it for others, but not for the self because of a belief in not being worthy. Wizardry is available but the fear of the unknown overrides the skill.

Ask Yourself: How do you avoid creating wizardry in your life? What are you capable of doing but don't believe you're good enough yet? Where did this belief come from? Is it time to tap into you own, innate knowing and become the Genius?

Symbolic: At this level, they are run by their passion; they live from their inner knowing and their connection with Source energy. It often means they have served a long apprenticeship to get there. They use creativity and bring forth new ideas. Merlin is an example of the Wizard Genius who brings forth the ancient skills of wizardry for the highest good of all.

WORRIER

Tribal: This is a dangerous archetype as it can lead to many illnesses. It's an addiction that runs our society cause of the programs we receive. Worry is misconstrued as compassion, but it just sends out negative energy. The only person it harms is the sender as it keeps the body in fear. The Worrier projects into the future where there is no power. The only real point of power is in the now moment.

Worry is a useless waste of energy at this level because it means you're living in fear. We usually have a role model to teach us how to worry; it is an acquired "skill." Of our own volition, we do not know how to worry, nor are we born worrying. But we are taught to see it as normal because everyone does it.

> *Ask Yourself: What do you worry about and why? Who taught you how to do this? Does it serve you? Why do you continue to worry when you know it's pointless? Does it ever change a situation by worrying about it?*

Symbolic: At this level, the Worrier takes its power back from the fear, comes into the present moment and has learned how to hold the vision of empowerment and trust. One understands about holding the vision for the bigger picture.

This means seeing the object of your worry as healthy, whole and healed. See this person in their integrity, walking their walk, living their truth and passion. Feel and know this person in alignment with their Higher Self guiding them always. There's no other vision to hold but this one. This is an empowered vision, not a fear based one, even if their physical reality shows you something else. It's using your intelligence to create a new world, not live in the old one that is addicted to fear.

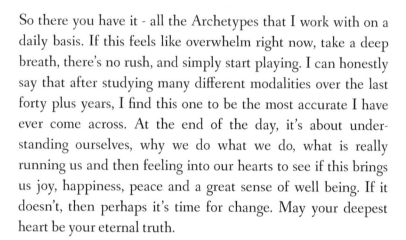

So there you have it - all the Archetypes that I work with on a daily basis. If this feels like overwhelm right now, take a deep breath, there's no rush, and simply start playing. I can honestly say that after studying many different modalities over the last forty plus years, I find this one to be the most accurate I have ever come across. At the end of the day, it's about understanding ourselves, why we do what we do, what is really running us and then feeling into our hearts to see if this brings us joy, happiness, peace and a great sense of well being. If it doesn't, then perhaps it's time for change. May your deepest heart be your eternal truth.

ABOUT THE AUTHOR

Barbara Stone-Andrews is a pioneer in the self-help industry having begun her own personal healing journey in 1976. She is a Reiki/Seichim Master, and successfully ran the Jamieson Sanctuary meditation retreat for many years, bringing empowerment, renewal, and healing to many thousands of people. Her studies with Dr. Caroline Myss, developed her love of Archetypes. Having personally conducted more than twenty thousand Archetype readings, Barbara is delighted to share her in-depth knowledge and guidance with people world wide through this book.

You can find her at www.archetypechartreadings.com where you can learn more about archetypes and have your own personal reading done.

Made in the USA
Monee, IL
10 April 2021